The Sales Manager's Guide to Developing a Winning Sales Team

CRITICAL TOOLS FOR OUTSTANDING RESULTS

Gerhard Gschwandtner
Founder and Publisher of *Selling Power*

McGraw·Hill

*New York   Chicago   San Francisco   Lisbon   London   Madrid   Mexico City
Milan   New Delhi   San Juan   Seoul   Singapore   Sydney   Toronto*

The McGraw·Hill Companies

Copyright ©2007 by Gerhard Gschwandter. All rights reserved. Printed in the United States of America. Except as permitted under the United States Copyright Act of 1976, no part of this publication may be reproduced or distributed in any form or by any means, or stored in a data base or retrieval system, without the prior written permission of the publisher.

1 2 3 4 5 6 7 8 9 0   DOC/DOC   0 9 8 7

ISBN-13: 978-0-07-147584-6
ISBN-10: 0-07-147584-2

McGraw-Hill books are available at special quantity discounts to use as premiums and sales promotions, or for use in corporate training programs. For more information, please write to the Director of Special Sales, Professional Publishing, McGraw-Hill, Two Penn Plaza, New York, NY 10121-2298. Or contact your local bookstore.

Contents

Introduction   v

Why You Need This Book to Develop High-Performing Salespeople   vii

PART ONE: The Manager's Problem Solver
Chapter 1: The Three Essential Success Factors   3
Chapter 2: Knowledge Review   17
Chapter 3: Skills Review   37
Chapter 4: Motivation Review   61

PART TWO: Essential Readings for Individual Growth

Essential Readings About Knowledge
Chapter 5: Getting Past Gatekeepers   85
Chapter 6: Generating Leads   91
Chapter 7: Perfecting Product Knowledge   95
Chapter 8: Outselling Your Competition   99
Chapter 9: Dealing with Difficult Customers   103

Chapter 10: Win–Win Negotiations 109
Chapter 11: Making the Most at Trade Shows 115
Chapter 12: Keys to Successful Travel 117

Essential Readings About Skills
Chapter 13: Cold Calling for Results 123
Chapter 14: E-mail as a Sales Tool 129
Chapter 15: Getting Attention with Sales Letters 135
Chapter 16: Leaving Effective Voice Mails 139
Chapter 17: Keys for Strong Communications 143
Chapter 18: Follow-up Strategies 147
Chapter 19: Writing Winning Proposals 153
Chapter 20: Handling Objections 157
Chapter 21: Closing Essentials 165
Chapter 22: Teleselling Skills 171
Chapter 23: Mastering Customer Service 177

Essential Readings About Motivation
Chapter 24: Ethics in Thought and Action 187
Chapter 25: Being a Professional in Every Way 195
Chapter 26: Working with Your Boss 199
Chapter 27: Keys to Self-Improvement 205
Chapter 28: Stress-Reduction Basics 211
Chapter 29: Always Strive for Success 215

Credits 219
Index 223

Introduction

The Sales Manager's Guide to Developing a Winning Sales Team has been created to help sales managers lead their salespeople through a rewarding process of ongoing sales improvement.

At the basis of this process is the assumption that a salesperson's success depends largely on three essential factors: *knowledge, skills,* and *motivation*. These success factors are within the salesperson's control and subject to the sales manager's influence.

In order to be successful in selling, salespeople have to develop all three major successful factors. Cumulative success requires not only ongoing improvement in each area but also a keen awareness of where improvement will pay off the most. *The Sales Manager's Guide to Developing a Winning Sales Team* has been designed to:

1. Create a dialogue between the salesperson and the sales manager with the goal of increasing the salesperson's awareness of his or her current level of Knowledge, skills, and motivation.
2. Uncover the salesperson's current performance gaps. These gaps will allow you to target future improvement efforts to those areas where improvement will be most beneficial.

3. Develop a realistic improvement plan for each area: knowledge, skills, and motivation. The improvement plan will include specific steps to be taken over the next three months and essential reading to improve crucial skills.
4. Establish a total score for the salesperson's current improvement potential. The total score is important for tracking future progress.
5. Provide a suitable reward for the salesperson for improving in all three areas: knowledge, skills, and motivation. If three months after the first review, the salesperson shows a minimum of 5 percent improvement in any of the three categories, he or she is entitled to receive a reward. A sales achievement certificate is attached to the back cover of this book. This award is to be presented to the salesperson by the sales manager.
6. Establish performance benchmarks for the entire sales team. A special summary review is enclosed to develop a combined performance rating for your entire sales team.
7. Provide effective coaching tools including Essential Readings on 25 different topics for the sales manager to ensure maximum success with this performance improvement tool.

Why You Need This Book to Develop High-Performing Salespeople

When the salesperson's performance is high, it is the salesperson who gets the credit; when the salesperson's performance is low, it is the sales manager who receives the blame.

Among all the problems a sales manager has to face, people problems are the toughest to handle. People problems cause sales managers to wear many hats.

When salespeople lack knowledge, the sales manager must wear the hat of a teacher.

When salespeople lack skills, the sales manager must wear the hat of a sales trainer.

When salespeople lack motivation, the sales manager has to wear the hat of a cheerleader, counselor, or amateur psychiatrist.

This book is designed to help you, the sales manager, become more proactive with solving sales performance problems. Instead of feeling overwhelmed by problems that are tough to sort out, you will feel a greater sense of control providing you apply this book consistently. As a result, you will be able to reduce your stress, and you will find managing your sales team more rewarding and more profitable.

PART ONE

The Manager's Problem Solver

CHAPTER ONE

The Three Essential Success Factors

Knowledge

Knowledge has become a critical factor in competing successfully.

Sales managers often overtrain their staff in the area of product knowledge and attempt to transform their salespeople into walking product encyclopedias. Although good product knowledge is a great asset in selling, it is not the only subject that salespeople need to master for reaching success.

To make a buying decision, today's customers demand more detailed information, and salespeople are expected to deliver this information quickly and accurately. As a result of changing customer requirements, salespeople need to know more than raw data; they must know where to obtain the right information and how to deliver the information to the customer in the shortest, most comprehensive, and most compelling way. Effective sales manager guide their sales people to acquire knowledge in all vital areas: knowledge of your company, your product, your customers, your industry, and your competition.

The two most critical challenges in managing sales knowledge are (1) keeping up-to-date with the latest information that is important to the customer and (2) keeping up-to-date with sales automation tools designed to enhance the communication process with customers. (This includes information management tools such as computers, modems, contact management programs, word processing programs, presentation software, etc.)

Given the rapid rate of change in sales knowledge and sales automation, sales managers must frequently measure the level of knowledge to prevent obsolescence. Effective sales managers will strive to achieve a healthy balance in their development efforts and give equal importance to increasing knowledge, improving selling skills, and increasing motivation.

Skills

There is no such thing as the "natural, born salesperson," like there is no "natural, born surgeon." Research has proven that good selling skills are the result of ongoing learning, professional coaching, and continuous practice.

Here are some of the skills sales professionals need to master in order to achieve any measure of success: prospecting, call preparation, listening, questioning, presentation, objection handling, and closing.

Selling skills are more difficult to measure than knowledge because they are subject to change. For example, a close that worked today on a sales call may not work tomorrow in a very similar situation. Like bacteria become resistant to certain antibiotics, customers become resistant to certain selling skills. Effective sales managers continually update their salespeople's range of skills to avid lost sales.

Whereas salespeople often claim to have many years of experience in selling, upon closer examination, their level of skills is nothing more than one year's worth of experience repeated over and over. There are no shortcuts to developing professional selling skills, and there are no shortcuts for measuring these skills. The best way to measure selling skills is through personal observation of the salesperson in action.

Poor sales managers often create a Catch 22 situation: They demand increased performance but they fail to measure skills. Because they never learn where improvement would be most beneficial, their salespeople are never given a chance to do better. These sales managers fail to realize that it is impossible to improve what we don't measure. This book will provide you with a simple, effective tool that will help you measure each salesperson's individual level of skills and develop a skills profile for your entire sales team.

Motivation

Without motivation, even the most knowledgeable or skilled salesperson can't win. A well-motivated salesperson has high expectations for achieving ambitious goals. Here are some of the motivational qualities of professional salespeople: enthusiasm, confidence, persistence, determination, discipline, and positive thinking. These qualities are easy to identify but tough to maintain over a long period of time. For example, many salespeople start in a new job with enthusiasm and determination, but within a few weeks they end up feeling down and discouraged.

What makes motivation so puzzling is that salespeople are often unaware of their own motivational difficulties. They say they are doing great when they actually could benefit from a good coaching session.

The biggest challenge is to create an environment in which salespeople can motivate themselves. Like a gardener plants seeds and pulls weeds, a sales manager has to perform similar functions to help salespeople grow.

A salesperson's motivation is like a plant in a garden. The plant has roots that can't be seen; they represent the salesperson's past, which can't be changed. Over a long period of time, the sales manager can help the salesperson create stronger roots (a stronger sense of identity or a stronger level of confidence). Like the stem of a plant moves toward the sunlight, salespeople tend to move toward challenging goals and attractive rewards. The sales manager has to help salespeople reach those goals and provide appropriate rewards. Like most plants have the capacity to bloom, most salespeople have the capacity to reach a profitable level of success. The sales manager's greatest challenge is to create the optimum motivational climate that encourages each salesperson's full talents to develop.

Common wisdom suggests that a salesperson respects what the sales manager expects and inspects.

The manager's expectation sets the standards, and the manager's enthusiasm is reflected in the hearts and minds of the sales team. When sales managers measure their salespeople's motivation, they must be prepared to see a partial reflection of themselves in the results.

How to Use the Sales Manager's Problem Solver

Use the problem solver in Part One of this book to grow the knowledge, skills, and motivation of each member of your sales team. Below are guidelines for using this amazing development tool.

1. Review by the Sales Manager

Read the entire book first in order to fully understand the subjects that you will be discussing with your salesperson. As you read about each subject to be evaluated, think of your salesperson's qualities and rate the salesperson's past performance using the rating scale described below.

2. Record Your Score

Open your book to Chapter Two, entitled "Knowledge Review," and begin evaluating your salesperson's performance in each area. Write your scores in the appropriate spaces using the rating scale described below. Use a #2 pencil. Only rate your salesperson in those areas that you are familiar with. If you are not sure of your rating, it is best to choose the "0" option (rating does not apply)

After you have gone through all three sections, set the book aside for a day. You will find that over a period of time, your thoughts about your salesperson's performance will crystallize and your final score will become more objective.

Here are two suggestions to help you complete those items that you were unable to rate:

(a) Spend some time with your salesperson to observe those areas that you were not 100 percent familiar with.
(b) Ask your sales training manager or another line manager for their input on certain (or all) areas.

3. Rating Scale

0 = Rating does not apply
1 = Lowest possible score (maximum improvement opportunity)

2 = Below average score (above average improvement opportunity)
3 = Average score (average improvement opportunity)
4 = Above average score (below average improvement opportunity)
5 = Maximum possible score (lowest possible improvement opportunity)

4. How to Rate Your Salespeople Objectively

Studies have shown that sales managers tend to evaluate their salespeople according to their own individual bias. For instance, sales managers who place a high value on relationships tend to see fewer opportunities for improvement than sales managers who place a high value on getting results. While the relationship-oriented manager may give the salesperson nothing lower than a four rating, the results-oriented manager may give the salesperson a one or a two (maximum improvement opportunity rating). In order to evaluate your salesperson objectively, keep these thoughts in mind:

1. Remember to separate the performance from the performer. You are not asked to rate the salesperson, but the salesperson's performance during the past three months. The salesperson's performance is not like a statue that's cast in bronze, it is more like a river that changes its currents and colors everyday.
2. Remember that the purpose of this exercise is to help your salespeople improve. The salesperson's ultimate improvement depends on four factors;

   - your ability to identify the opportunity for improvement;
   - the salesperson's ability to recognize the opportunity for improvement;

- your ability to coach the salesperson to achieve a higher performance level during the next three months;
- the salesperson's ability to learn and apply your coaching lessons.

3. Recognize that the way you evaluate your salesperson's past performance is not as important as the improvement process itself that you must implement—together with your salesperson. All past successes or failures are unimportant. what is most important is for you to develop a strong learning and development partnership with your salesperson. Tell your salesperson that no matter what "score" you settle on, this is a new beginning, the slate is clean, and the improvement process will start from this day forward. There is no finish line in the race for improvement.
4. Suggest to your salesperson not to be overly critical or overly generous in completing the evaluation. Explain that this review is just the first step of the ongoing improvement process and that you are not as much interested in today's results as in achieving improvement three months from today.
5. Please remember that this process should not be used as a power tool to "grade" (or degrade) your salespeople. There should be no link between this initial evaluation and compensation. There should be no reward or punishment as a result of performing this instrument. This management tool is designed to solve problems, not create new ones.

5. Prepare for the Review Meeting

Plan to spend at least one hour with your salesperson. It is preferable to choose a quite room, free of distractions or interruptions. (The ideal setting would be a neutral territory such as a conference room.)

It is important that you do not discuss your rating of the salesperson at this time. Save your comments until the salesperson has completed all three sections: knowledge, skills, and motivation.

6. Introduce the Review with a Prepared Statement

Here is a suggested summary statement for opening your meeting with the salesperson: "The purpose of this meeting is to help you grow as a sales professional. Over the next hour, we will be reviewing three major factors that lead to sales success: knowledge, skills, and motivation.

"Our goal is to find opportunities for improvement in all three areas. To make this review objective, fair, and productive, we'll both review the sales performance questions in this book. Your job is to rate your own performance. In the interest of achieving progress, it is important to be realistic in the appraisal of your current abilities. This instrument is designed to identify those areas in which you can benefit most from improvement, therefore the highest score is not automatically the best score.

"When you are finished, my job will be to compare your evaluation of yourself with my current evaluation of your past performance. Finally, we will identify the improvement opportunities in each area. This will be the basis for an improvement plan that we'll execute over the next three months. Three months from today, we'll review your progress and if you've met some of your goals, you will be presented with a sales achievement award in the next sales meeting."

7. The Sales Performance Review

Hand this book to your salesperson. Explain the rating scale and encourage the salesperson to be as objective as possible. Have a #2 pencil (with eraser) ready for the salesperson to use for recording the self-scoring process. Ask the salesperson to write his or her score into column 1. Let the salesperson know that it is not necessary to total the scores. Allow about 20 minutes for the salesperson to complete the review.

8. Develop the Combined Rating

After the salesperson has completed the review, write your own rating of the salesperson's performance in the appropriate spaces in column 2, then add up both scores to arrive at the "Combined Rating." Discuss the differences in your rating with the salesperson. Explain that it is okay to come up with different ratings. You may want to reassure the salesperson by saying, "If my rating is higher or lower than yours, there is no reason to worry, it only means that today I see more or less room for improvement than you do. What really counts is that we stay committed to ongoing improvement in all areas."

9. Identify the Improvement Opportunities

Compare the combined score with the maximum possible score, which is 10. To arrive at the "Improvement Opportunity" score, deduct your combined score from 10. For example, your combined score is 6, and the improvement opportunity is $10 - 6 = 4$.

10. Develop a Written Improvement Plan

At the end of each section (*knowledge*, *skills*, and *motivation*), you will find an easy-to-use improvement plan that contains the areas to be improved, actions to be taken, and a completion date for each step in your plan.

Get an agreement from your salesperson, and ask him or her to sign the completed improvement plan. Add your signature. Next, schedule a meeting date for the next review. Your salesperson may keep a copy of the improvement plan. Your may want to conclude your meeting with these words:

"Here is a summary of where you are today as a sales professional. We'll repeat this process three months from now. During the next three months, you have my commitment to help you improve in any way I can. I am confident that we'll both succeed with this plan. If your performance increases by at least 5 percent in any of these three categories, you will receive a special certificate. Thank you for your cooperation, and good luck."

11. Check Your Salesperson's Progress

Remember that the salesperson respects what the sales manager inspects. Monitor your salesperson's progress on a regular basis.

If coaching is part of the improvement plan, mark the dates in your calendar right after your meeting with the salesperson.

12. Repeat the Review Process After Three Months

Again, begin with reviewing each question carefully, and note your scores in the appropriate spaces in the book. Next, schedule a meeting with your salesperson and ask him or her to complete the review.

As in the first meeting, continue by adding the combined score and determine (a) how much improvement has taken place and (b) what areas of improvement remain to be worked on. Provide positive feedback to your salesperson for every score that has improved. Offer encouragement in case the salesperson's performance has slipped. Discuss the new performance gaps and work on a new plan for improvement. Next, calculate the improvement percentage in all three areas: knowledge, skills, and motivation. If the salesperson's performance has improved, promise to present the special certificate to the salesperson during your next sales meeting.

13. The Sales Achievement Certificate

The back of this book contains a special Personal Selling Power Certificate of Sales Achievement. This certificate was created to provide recognition for those salespeople whose performance rating has increased by at least 5 percent in any one of the three categories (knowledge, skills, and motivation) during the past three months. Make a copy of the certificate and type the salesperson's name in the appropriate space, add the date, the individual improvement percentages, and your signature. For greater impact, you may have this certificate framed at a local frame shop. In order to boost your salesperson's motivation, you may present this certificate during your next sales meeting.

COACHING TIPS

(Read this again prior to your meeting)

1. **Relax** Create a comfortable atmosphere of mutual respect.
2. **Focus clearly on your goal** If possible, do not put any other business matters on your agenda during this meeting (such as salary review, commission payments, vacation schedules, expense reports, sales forecast, etc.).

3. **Think about the psychological impact** Your scores can have great significance to the salesperson. Your job as the sales manager is to be friendly, relaxed, and supportive, yet to be firm with your expectations for improvement. Remember, in order to help the salesperson improve, you must help increase the salesperson's level of awareness. The two most obvious obstacles for raising awareness are to gloss over areas that need improving and to rigidly impose your score on the salesperson.

4. **Maintain an open attitude** Beware of your physical appearance. Avoid power gestures like leaning back with your hands folded behind your back or overly guarded gestures like folding your arms and crossing your legs away from your salesperson. Open gestures signal an open attitude, which will lead your salespeople to open up.

5. **Avoid sidetracking** Stay on course and move on at a steady pace. Listen carefully. If the salesperson keeps repeating the same theme over and over, remind him or her that you must move on and use the allotted time to discuss all areas.

6. **Be constructive: don't argue** Let's assume that your salesperson selected the highest possible score (5) for rating their closing skills and they are surprised that your score is much lower. Here are a few suggestions on how to handle the situation: Use clarifying questions like "Do you really feel that there is no way you could close more sales?" or "Can you explain the relationship between your closing skills and your sales results?" or "Do you realize that a score of five means that there is no room for improving your closing skills?"

Explain your reasoning. "I've observed your closing skills and I believe that you could benefit from sharpening them a little. If you'd like, we can cover this in greater detail when we discuss the improvement plan." Or, "I'd like to remind you that by giving yourself a 5 in this area, you are eliminating a chance for improvement. If your closing skills go up during the next three months, you may end up regretting your score today, because you won't be able to add improvement points." Remember that without a constructive dialogue, awareness is impossible. That is why this joint review should be conducted objectively, with respect for the salesperson's feelings and without discounting the sales manager's experience and insights.

7. **Resolve conflicts quickly** If conflicts arise, let the salesperson know that it is okay to disagree. Tell the salesperson, "We are allowed to disagree. Here is what we can do in this situation. We simply strike out this area from the review by selecting the zero score option. There are no consequences to you and you still qualify for the reward if your overall score moves up. Three months from now, we'll look at this again and I hope that by then we'll both be able to see things from the same perspective."

8. **Don't give up on your expectations** Remember that the ultimate goal of this review is not to impose your score on the salesperson, nor is it your role to rubber stamp the salesperson's score. It is natural for salespeople to fight awareness and resist improvement. When you encounter resistance, your insisting on immediate change will only be met with stiffer resistance. Your best way to help a reluctant salesperson is to temporarily accept the salesperson's

reluctance to change and repeat your expectations for improvement over the next three months.

Remember, we cannot control people, we can only influence their thinking. We can't mandate improvement, but we can resolve to never give up on our expectations. Like persistent salespeople get orders from resistant customers, persistent sales managers keep selling the benefits of change and in return get improvement from their salespeople.

9. **End on a positive note** Reassure the salesperson that you have faith in his or her ability to grow to a higher level of performance. Offer a fresh and positive outlook and share your bright vision of the salesperson's future. Your positive attitude is a powerful ingredient in the improvement process.

CHAPTER TWO
Knowledge Review

Rationale

Customers like to buy from salespeople who know their product. To the customer, a knowledgeable salesperson inspires confidence. In an increasingly complex world, knowledge translates into added value for the customer. The salesperson's knowledge often drives the customer's decision-making process. Whereas a lack of knowledge may turn customers to your competition, a high level of knowledge can act like a magnet that attracts more business.

Your Goal

To develop a fair, objective, and realistic profile of your salesperson's level of knowledge. Subjects covered:

1. Product knowledge
2. Application knowledge
3. Company knowledge

4. Industry knowledge
5. Customer knowledge
6. Competitive knowledge
7. Time and territory management
8. Sales automation and personal organization
9. Business rules and regulations
10. Professional development

Rating Scale

0 = Rating does not apply
1 = Lowest possible score (maximum improvement opportunity)
2 = Below average score (above average improvement opportunity)
3 = Average score (average improvement opportunity)
4 = Above average score (below average improvement opportunity)
5 = Maximum possible score (lowest possible improvement opportunity)

Note: Please feel free to expand (or decrease) the number of subjects covered as well as the number of questions within each subject.

KNOWLEDGE REVIEW

First Review / Second Review

	1	2	3	4	5	6	7	8	9	10	11
1 Product knowledge	Sales-person	Sales Manager	Combined Rating (Cols 1 + 2)	Ideal Score	Improvement Opportunity (Cols 4 - 3)	Sales-person	Sales Manager	Combined Rating (Cols 6 + 7)	Ideal Score	Improvement Opportunity (Cols 9 - 8)	Actual Improvement (Cols 10 - 5)
a) Knowledge of the essential features of our product and services	0 1 2 3 4 5	0 1 2 3 4 5		10		0 1 2 3 4 5	0 1 2 3 4 5		10		
b) Ability to translate all essential features into the appropriate customer benefits	0 1 2 3 4 5	0 1 2 3 4 5		10		0 1 2 3 4 5	0 1 2 3 4 5		10		
c) Ability to explain the financial advantages of our products and services to the customer	0 1 2 3 4 5	0 1 2 3 4 5		10		0 1 2 3 4 5	0 1 2 3 4 5		10		
d) Familiarity with all product promotions, sales manuals, and product literature	0 1 2 3 4 5	0 1 2 3 4 5		10		0 1 2 3 4 5	0 1 2 3 4 5		10		
e)	0 1 2 3 4 5	0 1 2 3 4 5		10		0 1 2 3 4 5	0 1 2 3 4 5		10		
f)	0 1 2 3 4 5	0 1 2 3 4 5		10		0 1 2 3 4 5	0 1 2 3 4 5		10		
Total product knowledge score:											

KNOWLEDGE REVIEW

2 Application knowledge

	First Review					Second Review					
	1 Sales-person	2 Sales Manager	3 Combined Rating (Cols 1 + 2)	4 Ideal Score	5 Improvement Opportunity (Cols 4 - 3)	6 Sales-person	7 Sales Manager	8 Combined Rating (Cols 6 + 7)	9 Ideal Score	10 Improvement Opportunity (Cols 9 - 8)	11 Actual Improvement (Cols 10 - 5)
a) Knowledge of how the product or service is used by the customer	0 1 2 3 4 5	0 1 2 3 4 5		10		0 1 2 3 4 5	0 1 2 3 4 5		10		
b) Knowledge of how the product is used by different customer groups	0 1 2 3 4 5	0 1 2 3 4 5		10		0 1 2 3 4 5	0 1 2 3 4 5		10		
c) Ability to understand the application from the customer's point of view	0 1 2 3 4 5	0 1 2 3 4 5		10		0 1 2 3 4 5	0 1 2 3 4 5		10		
d) Ability to understand the financial realities of using the product	0 1 2 3 4 5	0 1 2 3 4 5		10		0 1 2 3 4 5	0 1 2 3 4 5		10		
e)	0 1 2 3 4 5	0 1 2 3 4 5		10		0 1 2 3 4 5	0 1 2 3 4 5		10		
f)	0 1 2 3 4 5	0 1 2 3 4 5		10		0 1 2 3 4 5	0 1 2 3 4 5		10		
Total application knowledge score:											

KNOWLEDGE REVIEW

3 Company knowledge

	First Review					Second Review				
	1	2	3	4	5	6	7	8	9	10	11
	Sales-person	Sales Manager	Combined Rating (Cols 1 + 2)	Ideal Score	Improvement Opportunity (Cols 4 - 3)	Sales-person	Sales Manager	Combined Rating (Cols 6 + 7)	Ideal Score	Improvement Opportunity (Cols 9 - 8)	Actual Improvement (Cols 10 - 5)
a) Knowledge of your company's history, mission, and value	0 1 2 3 4 5	0 1 2 3 4 5		10		0 1 2 3 4 5	0 1 2 3 4 5		10		
b) Understanding of the company's policies, guidelines, and procedures	0 1 2 3 4 5	0 1 2 3 4 5		10		0 1 2 3 4 5	0 1 2 3 4 5		10		
c) Ability to tap into the knowledge and information resources within the company	0 1 2 3 4 5	0 1 2 3 4 5		10		0 1 2 3 4 5	0 1 2 3 4 5		10		
d) Ability to understand the financial realities of your company	0 1 2 3 4 5	0 1 2 3 4 5		10		0 1 2 3 4 5	0 1 2 3 4 5		10		
e)	0 1 2 3 4 5	0 1 2 3 4 5		10		0 1 2 3 4 5	0 1 2 3 4 5		10		
f)	0 1 2 3 4 5	0 1 2 3 4 5		10		0 1 2 3 4 5	0 1 2 3 4 5		10		
Total company knowledge score:											

KNOWLEDGE REVIEW

4 Industry knowledge

	First Review					Second Review					
	1 Sales-person	**2** Sales Manager	**3** Combined Rating (Cols 1 + 2)	**4** Ideal Score	**5** Improvement Opportunity (Cols 4 – 3)	**6** Sales-person	**7** Sales Manager	**8** Combined Rating (Cols 6 + 7)	**9** Ideal Score	**10** Improvement Opportunity (Cols 9 – 8)	**11** Actual Improvement (Cols 10 – 5)
a) Knowledge of industry associations and regulatory bodies	0 1 2 3 4 5	0 1 2 3 4 5		10		0 1 2 3 4 5	0 1 2 3 4 5		10		
b) Keeping up-to-date with current information on industry trends and developments	0 1 2 3 4 5	0 1 2 3 4 5		10		0 1 2 3 4 5	0 1 2 3 4 5		10		
c) Ability to understand the role of the key players in the industry and their influence	0 1 2 3 4 5	0 1 2 3 4 5		10		0 1 2 3 4 5	0 1 2 3 4 5		10		
d) Knowledge of all important trade shows and exhibits within the industry	0 1 2 3 4 5	0 1 2 3 4 5		10		0 1 2 3 4 5	0 1 2 3 4 5		10		
e)	0 1 2 3 4 5	0 1 2 3 4 5		10		0 1 2 3 4 5	0 1 2 3 4 5		10		
f)	0 1 2 3 4 5	0 1 2 3 4 5		10		0 1 2 3 4 5	0 1 2 3 4 5		10		
Total industry knowledge score:											

KNOWLEDGE REVIEW

5 Customer knowledge

	First Review					Second Review					
	1 Sales-person	2 Sales Manager	3 Combined Rating (Cols 1 + 2)	4 Ideal Score	5 Improvement Opportunity (Cols 4 - 3)	6 Sales-person	7 Sales Manager	8 Combined Rating (Cols 6 + 7)	9 Ideal Score	10 Improvement Opportunity (Cols 9 - 8)	11 Actual Improvement (Cols 10 - 5)
a) Ability to understand basic customer requirements	0 1 2 3 4 5	0 1 2 3 4 5		10		0 1 2 3 4 5	0 1 2 3 4 5		10		
b) Knowledge of our company's key customers as well as our customers' clients	0 1 2 3 4 5	0 1 2 3 4 5		10		0 1 2 3 4 5	0 1 2 3 4 5		10		
c) Ability to understand the financial realities of our customers' business	0 1 2 3 4 5	0 1 2 3 4 5		10		0 1 2 3 4 5	0 1 2 3 4 5		10		
d) Knowledge of the key decision makers within the customers' organizations	0 1 2 3 4 5	0 1 2 3 4 5		10		0 1 2 3 4 5	0 1 2 3 4 5		10		
e)	0 1 2 3 4 5	0 1 2 3 4 5		10		0 1 2 3 4 5	0 1 2 3 4 5		10		
f)	0 1 2 3 4 5	0 1 2 3 4 5		10		0 1 2 3 4 5	0 1 2 3 4 5		10		
Total customer knowledge score:											

KNOWLEDGE REVIEW

6 Competitive knowledge

	First Review					Second Review					
	1 Sales-person	2 Sales Manager	3 Combined Rating (Cols 1 + 2)	4 Ideal Score	5 Improvement Opportunity (Cols 4 − 3)	6 Sales-person	7 Sales Manager	8 Combined Rating (Cols 6 + 7)	9 Ideal Score	10 Improvement Opportunity (Cols 9 − 8)	11 Actual Improvement (Cols 10 − 5)
a) Knowledge of the top competitors' products and services	0 1 2 3 4 5	0 1 2 3 4 5		10		0 1 2 3 4 5	0 1 2 3 4 5		10		
b) Knowledge of the top competitors' key applications and prices	0 1 2 3 4 5	0 1 2 3 4 5		10		0 1 2 3 4 5	0 1 2 3 4 5		10		
c) Knowledge of the top competitors' sales and service strategies	0 1 2 3 4 5	0 1 2 3 4 5		10		0 1 2 3 4 5	0 1 2 3 4 5		10		
d) Ability to favorably compare our products and services to our competition	0 1 2 3 4 5	0 1 2 3 4 5		10		0 1 2 3 4 5	0 1 2 3 4 5		10		
e)	0 1 2 3 4 5	0 1 2 3 4 5		10		0 1 2 3 4 5	0 1 2 3 4 5		10		
f)	0 1 2 3 4 5	0 1 2 3 4 5		10		0 1 2 3 4 5	0 1 2 3 4 5		10		
Total industry knowledge score:											

KNOWLEDGE REVIEW

7 Time and territory management

	First Review					Second Review					
	1 Sales- person	**2** Sales Manager	**3** Combined Rating (Cols 1 + 2)	**4** Ideal Score	**5** Improvement Opportunity (Cols 4 - 3)	**6** Sales- person	**7** Sales Manager	**8** Combined Rating (Cols 6 + 7)	**9** Ideal Score	**10** Improvement Opportunity (Cols 9 - 8)	**11** Actual Improvement (Cols 10 - 5)
a) Ability to set daily goals and a realistic agenda for achieving these goals	0 1 2 3 4 5	0 1 2 3 4 5		10		0 1 2 3 4 5	0 1 2 3 4 5		10		
b) Ability to develop a productive list of calls, including prioritizing tasks	0 1 2 3 4 5	0 1 2 3 4 5		10		0 1 2 3 4 5	0 1 2 3 4 5		10		
c) Ability to meet deadlines and develop optimum number of contacts each week	0 1 2 3 4 5	0 1 2 3 4 5		10		0 1 2 3 4 5	0 1 2 3 4 5		10		
d) Ability to organize territory efficiently, keeping sales high and expenses low	0 1 2 3 4 5	0 1 2 3 4 5		10		0 1 2 3 4 5	0 1 2 3 4 5		10		
e)	0 1 2 3 4 5	0 1 2 3 4 5		10		0 1 2 3 4 5	0 1 2 3 4 5		10		
f)	0 1 2 3 4 5	0 1 2 3 4 5		10		0 1 2 3 4 5	0 1 2 3 4 5		10		
Total time and territory management score:											

KNOWLEDGE REVIEW

First Review | Second Review

8 Sales automation and personal organization	1 Sales-person	2 Sales Manager	3 Combined Rating (Cols 1 + 2)	4 Ideal Score	5 Improvement Opportunity (Cols 4 - 3)	6 Sales-person	7 Sales Manager	8 Combined Rating (Cols 6 + 7)	9 Ideal Score	10 Improvement Opportunity (Cols 9 - 8)	11 Actual Improvement (Cols 10 - 5)
a) Ability to use a computer for keeping track of prospects, appointments, and schedules	0 1 2 3 4 5	0 1 2 3 4 5		10		0 1 2 3 4 5	0 1 2 3 4 5		10		
b) Ability to write effective sales letters and provide quick response to customer inquiries	0 1 2 3 4 5	0 1 2 3 4 5		10		0 1 2 3 4 5	0 1 2 3 4 5		10		
c) Knowledge of basic software products to develop customized proposals	0 1 2 3 4 5	0 1 2 3 4 5		10		0 1 2 3 4 5	0 1 2 3 4 5		10		
d) Knowledge of software products to create sales presentations	0 1 2 3 4 5	0 1 2 3 4 5		10		0 1 2 3 4 5	0 1 2 3 4 5		10		
e)	0 1 2 3 4 5	0 1 2 3 4 5		10		0 1 2 3 4 5	0 1 2 3 4 5		10		
f)	0 1 2 3 4 5	0 1 2 3 4 5		10		0 1 2 3 4 5	0 1 2 3 4 5		10		
Total sales automation and organization score:											

KNOWLEDGE REVIEW

9. Business rules and regulations

Business rules and regulations	First Review					Second Review					
	1 Sales-person	2 Sales Manager	3 Combined Rating (Cols 1 + 2)	4 Ideal Score	5 Improvement Opportunity (Cols 4 - 3)	6 Sales-person	7 Sales Manager	8 Combined Rating (Cols 6 + 7)	9 Ideal Score	10 Improvement Opportunity (Cols 9 - 8)	11 Actual Improvement (Cols 10 - 5)
a) Knowledge of corporate code of ethics and industry standards	0 1 2 3 4 5	0 1 2 3 4 5		10		0 1 2 3 4 5	0 1 2 3 4 5		10		
b) Understanding of company policies and standard procedures governing sales	0 1 2 3 4 5	0 1 2 3 4 5		10		0 1 2 3 4 5	0 1 2 3 4 5		10		
c) Understanding of basic legal issues involved in entering sales contracts	0 1 2 3 4 5	0 1 2 3 4 5		10		0 1 2 3 4 5	0 1 2 3 4 5		10		
d) Ability to stay clear of potential legal conflicts; knowing when to ask for help	0 1 2 3 4 5	0 1 2 3 4 5		10		0 1 2 3 4 5	0 1 2 3 4 5		10		
e)	0 1 2 3 4 5	0 1 2 3 4 5		10		0 1 2 3 4 5	0 1 2 3 4 5		10		
f)	0 1 2 3 4 5	0 1 2 3 4 5		10		0 1 2 3 4 5	0 1 2 3 4 5		10		
Total business rules and regulations score:											

KNOWLEDGE REVIEW

10 Professional development

	First Review					Second Review					
	1 Sales-person	**2** Sales Manager	**3** Combined Rating (Cols 1 + 2)	**4** Ideal Score	**5** Improvement Opportunity (Cols 4 − 3)	**6** Sales-person	**7** Sales Manager	**8** Combined Rating (Cols 6 + 7)	**9** Ideal Score	**10** Improvement Opportunity (Cols 9 − 8)	**11** Actual Improvement (Cols 10 − 5)
a) Understanding of career goals and realistic plan for achieving them	0 1 2 3 4 5	0 1 2 3 4 5		10		0 1 2 3 4 5	0 1 2 3 4 5		10		
b) Enthusiastic commitment for ongoing professional improvement	0 1 2 3 4 5	0 1 2 3 4 5		10		0 1 2 3 4 5	0 1 2 3 4 5		10		
c) Personal commitment for increasing professional knowledge (1 hour/week minimum)	0 1 2 3 4 5	0 1 2 3 4 5		10		0 1 2 3 4 5	0 1 2 3 4 5		10		
d) Ability to teach other salespeople how to become more professional	0 1 2 3 4 5	0 1 2 3 4 5		10		0 1 2 3 4 5	0 1 2 3 4 5		10		
e)	0 1 2 3 4 5	0 1 2 3 4 5		10		0 1 2 3 4 5	0 1 2 3 4 5		10		
f)	0 1 2 3 4 5	0 1 2 3 4 5		10		0 1 2 3 4 5	0 1 2 3 4 5				
Total professional and development score:											

KNOWLEDGE REVIEW

	First Review					Second Review					
	1 Sales- person	**2** Sales Manager	**3** Combined Rating (Cols 1 + 2)	**4** Ideal Score	**5** Improvement Opportunity (Cols 4 - 3)	**6** Sales- person	**7** Sales Manager	**8** Combined Rating (Cols 6 + 7)	**9** Ideal Score	**10** Improvement Opportunity (Cols 9 - 8)	**11** Actual Improvement (Cols 10 - 5)
11 Additional category											
	0 1 2 3 4 5	0 1 2 3 4 5		10		0 1 2 3 4 5	0 1 2 3 4 5		10		
	0 1 2 3 4 5	0 1 2 3 4 5		10		0 1 2 3 4 5	0 1 2 3 4 5		10		
	0 1 2 3 4 5	0 1 2 3 4 5		10		0 1 2 3 4 5	0 1 2 3 4 5		10		
	0 1 2 3 4 5	0 1 2 3 4 5		10		0 1 2 3 4 5	0 1 2 3 4 5		10		
e)	0 1 2 3 4 5	0 1 2 3 4 5		10		0 1 2 3 4 5	0 1 2 3 4 5		10		
f)	0 1 2 3 4 5	0 1 2 3 4 5		10		0 1 2 3 4 5	0 1 2 3 4 5		10		
Total category score:											

Knowledge Review Summary	First Review	Second Review
Total salesperson score:		
Total sales manager score:		
Total combined rating:		
Total ideal score:		
Total improvement opportunity:		

Actual Improvement	
Improvement %	

Knowledge Improvement Plan

Please feel free to make a copy of this page for your salesperson.

_____ _____
Salesperson   Date

Areas to be improved	Actions to be taken	By when
1.		
2.		
3.		
4.		
5.		
6.		
7.		
8.		
9.		
10.		
11.		
12.		

_____ _____
Sales manager's signature   Salesperson's signature

Recommended Actions for Improving Sales Knowledge

1. Reading Assignments

Ask the salesperson to schedule time each week to read your company literature, study your sales manuals, scan industry journals, develop competitive comparisons, and read special books to fill the current knowledge gaps. In addition, the following Essential Readings in Part Two of the book will allow them to build their knowledge:

- Getting Past Gatekeepers
- Generating Leads
- Perfecting Product Knowledge
- Outselling Your Competition
- Dealing with Difficult Customers
- Win–Win Negotiations
- Making the Most at Trade Shows
- Keys to Successful Travel

2. Coaching and Consulting

Suggest that the salesperson meet with experts within your company such as your technical staff, your training department, your service department, and so forth. Explain the salesperson's knowledge goals to the internal coach or consultant. You may also choose a salesperson who scored high in the area of knowledge to help your salesperson improve.

3. Sales Training

Review your salesperson's level of performance with your sales training department. Your sales training manager may offer a special training session to a group of salespeople who have similar needs.

4. Self-Paced Training

You may suggest any available audiocassettes, videotapes or computer-guided self-training programs to help your salesperson fill the knowledge gaps.

5. Outside Training Programs

Your industry association or your local college may offer specialized courses to address your salespeople's needs for improved knowledge.

6. Visit the *Selling Power* Web Site

The *Selling Power* Web site is a valuable source of information. It can be found at www.sellingpower.com.

Knowledge Improvement Checklist

Complete this form three months after your initial review meeting.

1. Did salesperson complete the action plan 100 percent?
   ❑ Yes
   ❑ No
2. If you answered "No" to the above question, indicate reasons for not completing the action plan:

_____

_____

3. Did salesperson complete the action plan on time?
   ❑ Yes
   ❑ No
4. What was the total improvement opportunity? _____
5. What was the actual improvement score? _____
6. What was the improvement percentage? _____

To calculate the improvement percentage, multiply the actual improvement score (Column 11) by 100 and divide by the total improvement opportunity (Column 5). Ex: $20 \times 100 = 2000 \div 40 = 50\%$

7. If the improvement percentage is 5 percent or higher, enter the improvement percentage in the appropriate space of the sales achievement certificate at the end of this book.

How to Calculate and Use Your Team Score

The tool in this chapter can also allow you to determine the score for your entire team. To do this, fill out the Sales Team Performance Summary using the following instructions:

1. Add up each salesperson's score and add up your total team score.
2. Note the differences in knowledge within your sales team. Try to have those salespeople with high scores help those with the lowest scores.
3. Set a knowledge improvement goal for your entire sales team.
4. Measure your progress after three months. Compare the new score with the old score and determine your team improvement percentage.
5. Create a special group incentive to reward improved performance.

Sales Team Performance Summary Knowledge: First Review

Please transcribe the improvement opportunity scores (Column 10) of all your salespeople onto this page.   Date: _____

Name of Salesperson:											
1. Product knowledge											
2. Application knowledge											
3. Company knowledge											
4. Industry knowledge											
5. Customer knowledge											
6. Competitive knowledge											
7. Time and territory management											
8. Sales automation and personal organization											
9. Business rules and regulations											
10. Professional development											
11.											
Total sales team score – Knowledge:											

Sales Team Performance Summary Knowledge: Second Review

Please transcribe the improvement opportunity scores (Column 10) of all your salespeople onto this page.   Date: _____

Name of Salesperson:											
1. Product knowledge											
2. Application knowledge											
3. Company knowledge											
4. Industry knowledge											
5. Customer knowledge											
6. Competitive knowledge											
7. Time and territory management											
8. Sales automation and personal organization											
9. Business rules and regulations											
10. Professional development											
11.											
Total sales team score - Knowledge:											

CHAPTER THREE
Skills Review

Rationale

Customers prefer to do business with salespeople who demonstrate highly professional skills. In an increasingly competitive marketplace, products tend to become commodities, and skilled salespeople represent a significant competitive advantage. All selling skills can be divided into two major categories: relationship skills and sales process skills. While the salesperson's relationship skills create a positive climate for conducting business, sales process skills move the sale quickly from the opening to the close.

Your Goal

To develop a fair, objective, and realistic profile of your salesperson's professional skills. Subjects covered:

1. Prospecting skills
2. Relationship skills

3. Call-preparation skills
4. Consultative skills
5. Questioning skills
6. Listening skills
7. Presentation skills
8. Objection-handling skills
9. Personal persuasion skills
10. Closing skills
11. Follow-up skills
12. Advanced professional skills

Rating Scale

0 = Rating does not apply
1 = Lowest possible score (maximum improvement opportunity)
2 = Below average score (above average improvement opportunity)
3 = Average score (average improvement opportunity)
4 = Above average score (below average improvement opportunity)
5 = Maximum possible score (lowest possible improvement opportunity)

Note: Please feel free to expand (or decrease) the number of subjects covered as well as the number of questions within each subject.

SKILLS REVIEW

First Review | Second Review

	1 Sales-person	2 Sales Manager	3 Combined Rating (Cols 1 + 2)	4 Ideal Score	5 Improvement Opportunity (Cols 4 - 3)	6 Sales-person	7 Sales Manager	8 Combined Rating (Cols 6 + 7)	9 Ideal Score	10 Improvement Opportunity (Cols 9 - 8)	11 Actual Improvement (Cols 10 - 5)
1 Prospecting skills											
a) Ability to find new prospects from directories, guides, lists, etc.	0 1 2 3 4 5	0 1 2 3 4 5		10		0 1 2 3 4 5	0 1 2 3 4 5		10		
b) Ability to develop new prospects through referrals	0 1 2 3 4 5	0 1 2 3 4 5		10		0 1 2 3 4 5	0 1 2 3 4 5		10		
c) Ability to talk to anybody and ask for business leads	0 1 2 3 4 5	0 1 2 3 4 5		10		0 1 2 3 4 5	0 1 2 3 4 5		10		
d) Ability to follow the "sales funnel" system for replenishing the prospect base	0 1 2 3 4 5	0 1 2 3 4 5		10		0 1 2 3 4 5	0 1 2 3 4 5		10		
e)	0 1 2 3 4 5	0 1 2 3 4 5		10		0 1 2 3 4 5	0 1 2 3 4 5		10		
f)	0 1 2 3 4 5	0 1 2 3 4 5		10		0 1 2 3 4 5	0 1 2 3 4 5		10		
Total prospecting skills score:											

SKILLS REVIEW

2 Relationship skills

	First Review					Second Review					
	1 Sales- person	**2** Sales Manager	**3** Combined Rating (Cols 1 + 2)	**4** Ideal Score	**5** Improvement Opportunity (Cols 4 - 3)	**6** Sales- person	**7** Sales Manager	**8** Combined Rating (Cols 6 + 7)	**9** Ideal Score	**10** Improvement Opportunity (Cols 9 - 8)	**11** Actual Improvement (Cols 10 - 5)
a) Ability to create trust and rapport with any prospect	0 1 2 3 4 5	0 1 2 3 4 5		10		0 1 2 3 4 5	0 1 2 3 4 5		10		
b) Ability to create a relaxed and positive climate for selling	0 1 2 3 4 5	0 1 2 3 4 5		10		0 1 2 3 4 5	0 1 2 3 4 5		10		
c) Genuine desire to help other people through a win–win relationship	0 1 2 3 4 5	0 1 2 3 4 5		10		0 1 2 3 4 5	0 1 2 3 4 5		10		
d) Ability to treat each customer with respect, integrity, and a positive attitude	0 1 2 3 4 5	0 1 2 3 4 5		10		0 1 2 3 4 5	0 1 2 3 4 5		10		
e)	0 1 2 3 4 5	0 1 2 3 4 5		10		0 1 2 3 4 5	0 1 2 3 4 5		10		
f)	0 1 2 3 4 5	0 1 2 3 4 5		10		0 1 2 3 4 5	0 1 2 3 4 5		10		
Total relationship skills score:											

SKILLS REVIEW

First Review | Second Review

3 Call-preparation skills	1 Sales-person	2 Sales Manager	3 Combined Rating (Cols 1 + 2)	4 Ideal Score	5 Improvement Opportunity (Cols 4 - 3)	6 Sales-person	7 Sales Manager	8 Combined Rating (Cols 6 + 7)	9 Ideal Score	10 Improvement Opportunity (Cols 9 - 8)	11 Actual Improvement (Cols 10 - 5)
a) Ability to schedule sales calls at the right time with the right decision-maker(s)	0 1 2 3 4 5	0 1 2 3 4 5		10		0 1 2 3 4 5	0 1 2 3 4 5		10		
b) Preparation of literature, testimonials, visual aids, sales contracts, etc.	0 1 2 3 4 5	0 1 2 3 4 5		10		0 1 2 3 4 5	0 1 2 3 4 5		10		
c) Advance knowledge of the customer's particular situation	0 1 2 3 4 5	0 1 2 3 4 5		10		0 1 2 3 4 5	0 1 2 3 4 5		10		
d) Use of a specific objective for each sales call	0 1 2 3 4 5	0 1 2 3 4 5		10		0 1 2 3 4 5	0 1 2 3 4 5		10		
e)	0 1 2 3 4 5	0 1 2 3 4 5		10		0 1 2 3 4 5	0 1 2 3 4 5		10		
f)	0 1 2 3 4 5	0 1 2 3 4 5		10		0 1 2 3 4 5	0 1 2 3 4 5		10		
Total call-preparation skills score:											

SKILLS REVIEW	First Review					Second Review					
	1	2	3	4	5	6	7	8	9	10	11
4 Consultative skills	Sales-person	Sales Manager	Combined Rating (Cols 1 + 2)	Ideal Score	Improvement Opportunity (Cols 4 - 3)	Sales-person	Sales Manager	Combined Rating (Cols 6 + 7)	Ideal Score	Improvement Opportunity (Cols 9 - 8)	Actual Improvement (Cols 10 - 5)
a) Ability to diagnose customer needs fast and accurately	0 1 2 3 4 5	0 1 2 3 4 5		10		0 1 2 3 4 5	0 1 2 3 4 5		10		
b) Ability to understand and appreciate the customer's point of view	0 1 2 3 4 5	0 1 2 3 4 5		10		0 1 2 3 4 5	0 1 2 3 4 5		10		
c) Ability to form a reliable partnership with the customer	0 1 2 3 4 5	0 1 2 3 4 5		10		0 1 2 3 4 5	0 1 2 3 4 5		10		
d) Ability to engage and involve the customer at every step of the sales process	0 1 2 3 4 5	0 1 2 3 4 5		10		0 1 2 3 4 5	0 1 2 3 4 5		10		
e)	0 1 2 3 4 5	0 1 2 3 4 5		10		0 1 2 3 4 5	0 1 2 3 4 5		10		
f)	0 1 2 3 4 5	0 1 2 3 4 5		10		0 1 2 3 4 5	0 1 2 3 4 5		10		
Total consultative skills score:											

SKILLS REVIEW	First Review					Second Review					
	1	2	3	4	5	6	7	8	9	10	11
5 **Questioning skills**	Sales-person	Sales Manager	Combined Rating (Cols 1 + 2)	Ideal Score	Improvement Opportunity (Cols 4 - 3)	Sales-person	Sales Manager	Combined Rating (Cols 6 + 7)	Ideal Score	Improvement Opportunity (Cols 9 - 8)	Actual Improvement (Cols 10 - 5)
a) Ability to develop interesting and compelling sales questions	0 1 2 3 4 5	0 1 2 3 4 5		10		0 1 2 3 4 5	0 1 2 3 4 5		10		
b) Ability to find out more than what the customer originally planned to tell	0 1 2 3 4 5	0 1 2 3 4 5		10		0 1 2 3 4 5	0 1 2 3 4 5		10		
c) Ability to lead the customer to discover the advantages of your company's products	0 1 2 3 4 5	0 1 2 3 4 5		10		0 1 2 3 4 5	0 1 2 3 4 5		10		
help the customer face tough choices without losing control of the sale	0 1 2 3 4 5	0 1 2 3 4 5		10		0 1 2 3 4 5	0 1 2 3 4 5		10		
e)	0 1 2 3 4 5	0 1 2 3 4 5		10		0 1 2 3 4 5	0 1 2 3 4 5		10		
f)	0 1 2 3 4 5	0 1 2 3 4 5		10		0 1 2 3 4 5	0 1 2 3 4 5				
Total questioning skills score:											

SKILLS REVIEW

6 Listening skills

	First Review					Second Review					
	1 Sales-person	**2** Sales Manager	**3** Combined Rating (Cols 1 + 2)	**4** Ideal Score	**5** Improvement Opportunity (Cols 4 - 3)	**6** Sales-person	**7** Sales Manager	**8** Combined Rating (Cols 6 + 7)	**9** Ideal Score	**10** Improvement Opportunity (Cols 9 - 8)	**11** Actual Improvement (Cols 10 - 5)
a) Ability to listen for facts, feelings, and priorities during a sales call	0 1 2 3 4 5	0 1 2 3 4 5		10		0 1 2 3 4 5	0 1 2 3 4 5		10		
b) Ability to hold back the urge to talk and to take notes while the customer talks	0 1 2 3 4 5	0 1 2 3 4 5		10		0 1 2 3 4 5	0 1 2 3 4 5		10		
c) Ability to summarize, rephrase, and paraphrase the customer's statements	0 1 2 3 4 5	0 1 2 3 4 5		10		0 1 2 3 4 5	0 1 2 3 4 5		10		
d) Ability to develop a complete proposal that reflects the customer's needs 100 percent	0 1 2 3 4 5	0 1 2 3 4 5		10		0 1 2 3 4 5	0 1 2 3 4 5		10		
e)	0 1 2 3 4 5	0 1 2 3 4 5		10		0 1 2 3 4 5	0 1 2 3 4 5		10		
f)	0 1 2 3 4 5	0 1 2 3 4 5		10		0 1 2 3 4 5	0 1 2 3 4 5		10		
Total listening skills score:											

SKILLS REVIEW

7 Presentation skills

	First Review					Second Review					
	1	2	3	4	5	6	7	8	9	10	11
	Sales-person	Sales Manager	Combined Rating (Cols 1 + 2)	Ideal Score	Improvement Opportunity (Cols 4 − 3)	Sales-person	Sales Manager	Combined Rating (Cols 6 + 7)	Ideal Score	Improvement Opportunity (Cols 9 − 8)	Actual Improvement (Cols 10 − 5)
a) Ability to prepare a comprehensive and persuasive sales presentation	0 1 2 3 4 5	0 1 2 3 4 5		10		0 1 2 3 4 5	0 1 2 3 4 5		10		
b) Ability to use visual aids, presentation products—hardware and/or software	0 1 2 3 4 5	0 1 2 3 4 5		10		0 1 2 3 4 5	0 1 2 3 4 5		10		
c) Ability to talk freely and confidently to a group of customers	0 1 2 3 4 5	0 1 2 3 4 5		10		0 1 2 3 4 5	0 1 2 3 4 5		10		
d) Ability to translate product features into relevant customer benefits	0 1 2 3 4 5	0 1 2 3 4 5		10		0 1 2 3 4 5	0 1 2 3 4 5		10		
e)	0 1 2 3 4 5	0 1 2 3 4 5		10		0 1 2 3 4 5	0 1 2 3 4 5		10		
f)	0 1 2 3 4 5	0 1 2 3 4 5		10		0 1 2 3 4 5	0 1 2 3 4 5				
Total presentation skills score:											

SKILLS REVIEW

8 Objection-handling skills

	First Review					Second Review						
	1 Sales-person	**2** Sales Manager	**3** Combined Rating (Cols 1 + 2)	**4** Ideal Score	**5** Improvement Opportunity (Cols 4 – 3)	**6** Sales-person	**7** Sales Manager	**8** Combined Rating (Cols 6 + 7)	**9** Ideal Score	**10** Improvement Opportunity (Cols 9 – 8)	**11** Actual Improvement (Cols 10 – 5)
a) Ability to anticipate customer objection before they become a problem	0 1 2 3 4 5	0 1 2 3 4 5		10		0 1 2 3 4 5	0 1 2 3 4 5		10		
b) Ability to empathize with the customer and clearly isolate the real objection	0 1 2 3 4 5	0 1 2 3 4 5		10		0 1 2 3 4 5	0 1 2 3 4 5		10		
c) Ability to defuse the objection in a number of different ways that solve the real problem	0 1 2 3 4 5	0 1 2 3 4 5		10		0 1 2 3 4 5	0 1 2 3 4 5		10		
d) Ability to meet all selling obstacles in an open and constructive way	0 1 2 3 4 5	0 1 2 3 4 5		10		0 1 2 3 4 5	0 1 2 3 4 5		10		
e)	0 1 2 3 4 5	0 1 2 3 4 5		10		0 1 2 3 4 5	0 1 2 3 4 5		10		
f)	0 1 2 3 4 5	0 1 2 3 4 5		10		0 1 2 3 4 5	0 1 2 3 4 5		10		
Total objection-handling skills score:											

SKILLS REVIEW	First Review					Second Review					
	1	2	3	4	5	6	7	8	9	10	11
9) Personal persuasion skills	Sales-person	Sales Manager	Combined Rating (Cols 1 + 2)	Ideal Score	Improvement Opportunity (Cols 4 - 3)	Sales-person	Sales Manager	Combined Rating (Cols 6 + 7)	Ideal Score	Improvement Opportunity (Cols 9 - 8)	Actual Improvement (Cols 10 - 5)
a) Appropriate dress and appearance in selling to a diverse group of customers	0 1 2 3 4 5	0 1 2 3 4 5		10		0 1 2 3 4 5	0 1 2 3 4 5		10		
b) Ability to adapt to a wide range of challenging prospects	0 1 2 3 4 5	0 1 2 3 4 5		10		0 1 2 3 4 5	0 1 2 3 4 5		10		
c) Ability to speak clearly, persuasively, and enthusiastically to any prospect	0 1 2 3 4 5	0 1 2 3 4 5		10		0 1 2 3 4 5	0 1 2 3 4 5		10		
d) Ability to use effective nonverbal communication techniques (positive gestures, posture, etc.)	0 1 2 3 4 5	0 1 2 3 4 5		10		0 1 2 3 4 5	0 1 2 3 4 5		10		
e)	0 1 2 3 4 5	0 1 2 3 4 5		10		0 1 2 3 4 5	0 1 2 3 4 5		10		
f)	0 1 2 3 4 5	0 1 2 3 4 5		10		0 1 2 3 4 5	0 1 2 3 4 5		10		
Total personal persuasion skills score:											

SKILLS REVIEW

10 Closing skills

	First Review					Second Review					
	1 Sales-person	**2** Sales Manager	**3** Combined Rating (Cols 1 + 2)	**4** Ideal Score	**5** Improvement Opportunity (Cols 4 – 3)	**6** Sales-person	**7** Sales Manager	**8** Combined Rating (Cols 6 + 7)	**9** Ideal Score	**10** Improvement Opportunity (Cols 9 – 8)	**11** Actual Improvement (Cols 10 – 5)
a) Ability to ask for the close at least three times	0 1 2 3 4 5	0 1 2 3 4 5		10		0 1 2 3 4 5	0 1 2 3 4 5		10		
b) Ability to master at least five different closing techniques	0 1 2 3 4 5	0 1 2 3 4 5		10		0 1 2 3 4 5	0 1 2 3 4 5		10		
c) Ability to negotiate for the best possible terms of the sale (price, payment, delivery)	0 1 2 3 4 5	0 1 2 3 4 5		10		0 1 2 3 4 5	0 1 2 3 4 5		10		
d) Ability to keep the sale closed once the order is signed	0 1 2 3 4 5	0 1 2 3 4 5		10		0 1 2 3 4 5	0 1 2 3 4 5		10		
e)	0 1 2 3 4 5	0 1 2 3 4 5		10		0 1 2 3 4 5	0 1 2 3 4 5		10		
f)	0 1 2 3 4 5	0 1 2 3 4 5		10		0 1 2 3 4 5	0 1 2 3 4 5				
Total closing skills score:											

SKILLS REVIEW

First Review | Second Review

11 **Follow-up skills**	1 Sales-person	2 Sales Manager	3 Combined Rating (Cols 1 + 2)	4 Ideal Score	5 Improvement Opportunity (Cols 4 - 3)	6 Sales-person	7 Sales Manager	8 Combined Rating (Cols 6 + 7)	9 Ideal Score	10 Improvement Opportunity (Cols 9 - 8)	11 Actual Improvement (Cols 10 - 5)
a) Ability to upsell customer after the sale is closed	0 1 2 3 4 5	0 1 2 3 4 5		10		0 1 2 3 4 5	0 1 2 3 4 5		10		
b) Ability to ask for referrals after the product or service has been delivered	0 1 2 3 4 5	0 1 2 3 4 5		10		0 1 2 3 4 5	0 1 2 3 4 5		10		
c) Ability to expand the relationship with the customer and probe for additional needs	0 1 2 3 4 5	0 1 2 3 4 5		10		0 1 2 3 4 5	0 1 2 3 4 5		10		
d) Ability to get customer testimonials to facilitate sales to new prospects	0 1 2 3 4 5	0 1 2 3 4 5		10		0 1 2 3 4 5	0 1 2 3 4 5		10		
e)	0 1 2 3 4 5	0 1 2 3 4 5		10		0 1 2 3 4 5	0 1 2 3 4 5		10		
f)	0 1 2 3 4 5	0 1 2 3 4 5		10		0 1 2 3 4 5	0 1 2 3 4 5		10		
Total follow-up skills score:											

SKILLS REVIEW

First Review | Second Review

	1	2	3	4	5	6	7	8	9	10	11
12 Advanced professional skills	Sales-person	Sales Manager	Combined Rating (Cols 1 + 2)	Ideal Score	Improvement Opportunity (Cols 4 - 3)	Sales-person	Sales Manager	Combined Rating (Cols 6 + 7)	Ideal Score	Improvement Opportunity (Cols 9 - 8)	Actual Improvement (Cols 10 - 5)
a) Ability to lead a team of people from your company to work with the customer's team	0 1 2 3 4 5	0 1 2 3 4 5		10		0 1 2 3 4 5	0 1 2 3 4 5		10		
b) Ability to assist the sales manager in training and coaching new salespeople	0 1 2 3 4 5	0 1 2 3 4 5		10		0 1 2 3 4 5	0 1 2 3 4 5		10		
c) Ability to organize sales campaigns, trade shows, or open-house events	0 1 2 3 4 5	0 1 2 3 4 5		10		0 1 2 3 4 5	0 1 2 3 4 5		10		
d) Ability to develop sales literature, sales manuals, or new marketing ideas	0 1 2 3 4 5	0 1 2 3 4 5		10		0 1 2 3 4 5	0 1 2 3 4 5		10		
e)	0 1 2 3 4 5	0 1 2 3 4 5		10		0 1 2 3 4 5	0 1 2 3 4 5		10		
f)	0 1 2 3 4 5	0 1 2 3 4 5		10		0 1 2 3 4 5	0 1 2 3 4 5		10		
Total advanced professional skills score:											

SKILLS REVIEW

11 Additional category

	First Review					Second Review						
	1 Sales-person	**2** Sales Manager	**3** Combined Rating (Cols 1 + 2)	**4** Ideal Score	**5** Improvement Opportunity (Cols 4 − 3)	**6** Sales-person	**7** Sales Manager	**8** Combined Rating (Cols 6 + 7)	**9** Ideal Score	**10** Improvement Opportunity (Cols 9 − 8)	**11** Actual Improvement (Cols 10 − 5)
	0 1 2 3 4 5	0 1 2 3 4 5		10		0 1 2 3 4 5	0 1 2 3 4 5		10		
	0 1 2 3 4 5	0 1 2 3 4 5		10		0 1 2 3 4 5	0 1 2 3 4 5		10		
	0 1 2 3 4 5	0 1 2 3 4 5		10		0 1 2 3 4 5	0 1 2 3 4 5		10		
	0 1 2 3 4 5	0 1 2 3 4 5		10							
e)	0 1 2 3 4 5	0 1 2 3 4 5		10		0 1 2 3 4 5	0 1 2 3 4 5		10		
f)	0 1 2 3 4 5	0 1 2 3 4 5		10		0 1 2 3 4 5	0 1 2 3 4 5		10		
Total category score:											

Skills Review Summary	First Review	Second Review	Actual Improvement
Total salesperson score:			
Total sales manager score:			
Total combined rating:			
Total ideal score:			
Total improvement opportunity:			

Improvement %

Skills Improvement Plan

Please feel free to make a copy of this page for your salesperson.

Salesperson _____   Date _____

Areas to be improved	Actions to be taken	By when
1.		
2.		
3.		
4.		
5.		
6.		
7.		
8.		
9.		
10.		
11.		
12.		

Sales manager's signature _____   Salesperson's signature _____

Recommended Actions for Improving Sales Skills

1. Reading Assignments

Bookstores and libraries are full of excellent books that you may recommend to your salespeople for improving their professional selling skills. These books should be part of any good sales office library. In addition, the following Essential Readings in Part Two cover key skills for every sales professsional:

- Cold Calling for Results
- E-mail as a Sales Tool
- Getting Attention with Sales Letters
- Leaving Effective Voice Mails
- Keys for Strong Communications
- Follow-up Strategies
- Writing Winning Proposals
- Handling Objections
- Closing Essentials
- Teleselling Skills
- Mastering Customer Service

2. Audio and Video Training

There are many valuable audio and video programs that can help your salespeople improve their skills. Consider getting a catalog from Nightingale-Conant (800) 525-9000, one of the leading publishers of sales skills and motivation programs.

3. In-house Sales Training

Chances are that your in-house training department is the best resource for your salesperson to develop the highest level of selling skills. To make training pay off, be sure to get your sales trainer involved in your sales performance review. Also, after the salesperson has completed the skills training course, give your sales trainer feedback on the results. Remember that skills atrophy without practice. Make skills training a regular part of your sales meetings. Note: The Dartnell Corporation distributes a series of education sales training films for in-house training. Call (800) 621-5463 for a catalog.

4. One-on-One Coaching

Set a day aside for making joint calls with your salesperson. Before each call, review the call objective and the actions to be taken during the call, and discuss the possible scenarios for dealing with the customer. During the call, take a more neutral role, assist if it is advisable, and observe the salesperson's skills in action. After the call, review the salesperson's performance. Always ask the salesperson first, "If you had to do this over again, what would you do differently?" Then offer your constructive feedback. First, state what you liked about the salesperson's performance, next, explain what you would have done differently and describe how.

5. Outside Sales Training Courses

Chances are that there are a number of seminars and sales training courses offered by your industry trade association. In addition, there are many training companies, associations, and independent sales training consultants that offer selling skills training programs.

6. College Courses

There are many colleges that offer professional selling skills courses at a very reasonable rate to sales professionals. Ask your salesperson to check into the programs available in his or her community.

7. Visit the Selling Power Web Site

www.sellingpower.com

Skills Improvement Checklist

Complete this form three months after your initial review meeting.

1. Did salesperson complete the action plan 100 percent?
   - ❏ Yes
   - ❏ No

2. If you answered "No" to the above question, indicate reasons for not completing the action plan:

   _____

   _____

3. Did salesperson complete the action plan on time?
   - ❏ Yes
   - ❏ No

4. What was the total improvement opportunity? _____

5. What was the actual improvement score? _____

6. What was the improvement percentage? _____

To calculate the improvement percentage, multiply the actual improvement score (Column 11) by 100 and divide by the total improvement opportunity (Column 5). Ex: $20 \times 100 = 2000 \div 40 = 50\%$

7. If the improvement percentage is 5 percent or higher, enter the improvement percentage in the appropriate space of the sales achievement certificate at the end of this book.

How to Calculate and Use Your Team Score

To assess the skill level of your entire team, the Sales Team Performance Summary allows you to record the improvement of each team member's skill performance. Use the following steps as you fill out this review.

1. Add up each salesperson's score and add up your total team score.
2. Note the differences in knowledge within your sales team. Try to have those salespeople with high scores help those with the lowest scores.
3. Set a knowledge improvement goal for your entire sales team.
4. Measure your progress after three months. Compare the new score with to the old score and determine your team improvement percentage.
5. Create a special group incentive to reward improved performance.

Sales Team Performance Summary Skills: First Review

Please transcribe the improvement opportunity scores (Column 10) of all your salespeople onto this page. Date: _____

Name of Salesperson:											
1. Prospecting skills											
2. Relationship skills											
3. Call-preparation skills											
4. Consultative skills											
5. Questioning skills											
6. Listening skills											
7. Presentation skills											
8. Objection-handling skills											
9. Personal persuasion skills											
10. Closing skills											
11. Follow-up skills											
12. Advanced professional skills											
13.											
Total sales team score — Skills											

Sales Team Performance Summary Skills: Second Review

Please transcribe the improvement opportunity scores (Column 10) of all your salespeople onto this page.   Date: _____

Name of Salesperson:												
1. Prospecting skills												
2. Relationship skills												
3. Call-preparation skills												
4. Consultative skills												
5. Questioning skills												
6. Listening skills												
7. Presentation skills												
8. Objection-handling skills												
9. Personal persuasion skills												
10. Closing skills												
11. Follow-up skills												
12. Advanced professional skills												
13.												
Total sales team score – Skills												

CHAPTER FOUR
Motivation Review

Rationale

Motivated salespeople attract more customers in a day than demotivated people can persuade in a month. But motivation without skills or knowledge rarely leads to a closed sale. The most successful salespeople are knowledgeable, skilled, *and* motivated. All motivation begins with self-motivation. It begins with the inner desire to help customers, to find meaning in creating satisfied customers, to love the freedom and independence of the profession, to get excited at the prospect of winning, to be enthusiastic about each small victory, and to keep going after each major defeat.

Your Goal

To develop a fair, objective, and realistic profile of your salesperson's level of motivation. Subjects covered:

1. Positive thinking
2. Enthusiasm

3. Self-confidence
4. Desire to win
5. Persistence and discipline
6. Handling rejection and failure
7. Managing disappointment
8. Positive living
9. Exercise and stress management
10. Finding meaning and fulfillment

Rating Scale

0 = Rating does not apply
1 = Lowest possible score (maximum improvement opportunity)
2 = Below average score (above average improvement opportunity)
3 = Average score (average improvement opportunity)
4 = Above average score (below average improvement opportunity)
5 = Maximum possible score (lowest possible improvement opportunity)

Note: Please feel free to expand (or decrease) the number of subjects covered as well as the number of question within each subject.

MOTIVATION REVIEW

1 Positive thinking

	First Review					Second Review						
	1	2	3	4	5	6	7	8	9	10	11
	Sales-person	Sales Manager	Combined Rating (Cols 1 + 2)	Ideal Score	Improvement Opportunity (Cols 4 − 3)	Sales-person	Sales Manager	Combined Rating (Cols 6 + 7)	Ideal Score	Improvement Opportunity (Cols 9 − 8)	Actual Improvement (Cols 10 − 5)
a) Ongoing interest in positive literature, success stories, and cassettes	0 1 2 3 4 5	0 1 2 3 4 5		10		0 1 2 3 4 5	0 1 2 3 4 5		10		
b) Ability to see the best in each situation; always looking at the bright side	0 1 2 3 4 5	0 1 2 3 4 5		10		0 1 2 3 4 5	0 1 2 3 4 5		10		
c) Ability to seek out positive role models and form relationships with winners	0 1 2 3 4 5	0 1 2 3 4 5		10		0 1 2 3 4 5	0 1 2 3 4 5		10		
d) Ability to think optimistically about the company, the economy, and the future	0 1 2 3 4 5	0 1 2 3 4 5		10		0 1 2 3 4 5	0 1 2 3 4 5		10		
e)	0 1 2 3 4 5	0 1 2 3 4 5		10		0 1 2 3 4 5	0 1 2 3 4 5		10		
f)	0 1 2 3 4 5	0 1 2 3 4 5		10		0 1 2 3 4 5	0 1 2 3 4 5				
Total positive thinking score:											

MOTIVATION REVIEW

2 Enthusiasm

	First Review					Second Review					
	1 Sales-person	**2** Sales Manager	**3** Combined Rating (Cols 1 + 2)	**4** Ideal Score	**5** Improvement Opportunity (Cols 4 - 3)	**6** Sales-person	**7** Sales Manager	**8** Combined Rating (Cols 6 + 7)	**9** Ideal Score	**10** Improvement Opportunity (Cols 9 - 8)	**11** Actual Improvement (Cols 10 - 5)
a) Ability to get excited about the product, the company, and new selling challenges	0 1 2 3 4 5	0 1 2 3 4 5		10		0 1 2 3 4 5	0 1 2 3 4 5		10		
b) Ability to work with enthusiasm, spreading good cheer among people	0 1 2 3 4 5	0 1 2 3 4 5		10		0 1 2 3 4 5	0 1 2 3 4 5		10		
c) Ability to go the extra mile for the customer and shoulder extra duties without complaint	0 1 2 3 4 5	0 1 2 3 4 5		10		0 1 2 3 4 5	0 1 2 3 4 5		10		
d) Ability to view obstacles as exciting challenges for learning	0 1 2 3 4 5	0 1 2 3 4 5		10		0 1 2 3 4 5	0 1 2 3 4 5		10		
e)	0 1 2 3 4 5	0 1 2 3 4 5		10		0 1 2 3 4 5	0 1 2 3 4 5		10		
f)	0 1 2 3 4 5	0 1 2 3 4 5		10		0 1 2 3 4 5	0 1 2 3 4 5				
Total enthusiasm score:											

MOTIVATION REVIEW

First Review | Second Review

	1	2	3	4	5	6	7	8	9	10	11
3 Self-confidence	Sales-person	Sales Manager	Combined Rating (Cols 1 + 2)	Ideal Score	Improvement Opportunity (Cols 4 - 3)	Sales-person	Sales Manager	Combined Rating (Cols 6 + 7)	Ideal Score	Improvement Opportunity (Cols 9 - 8)	Actual Improvement (Cols 10 - 5)
a) Ability to develop high self-esteem even during difficult times	0 1 2 3 4 5	0 1 2 3 4 5		10		0 1 2 3 4 5	0 1 2 3 4 5		10		
b) Ability to maintain grace under highly stressful situations	0 1 2 3 4 5	0 1 2 3 4 5		10		0 1 2 3 4 5	0 1 2 3 4 5		10		
c) Ability to readily admit mistakes and learn from failures	0 1 2 3 4 5	0 1 2 3 4 5		10		0 1 2 3 4 5	0 1 2 3 4 5		10		
d) Ability to seek competent help when unusual problems arise	0 1 2 3 4 5	0 1 2 3 4 5		10		0 1 2 3 4 5	0 1 2 3 4 5		10		
e)	0 1 2 3 4 5	0 1 2 3 4 5		10		0 1 2 3 4 5	0 1 2 3 4 5		10		
f)	0 1 2 3 4 5	0 1 2 3 4 5		10		0 1 2 3 4 5	0 1 2 3 4 5		10		
Total self-confidence score:											

MOTIVATION REVIEW	First Review					Second Review					
	1	2	3	4	5	6	7	8	9	10	11
4 Desire to win	Sales-person	Sales Manager	Combined Rating (Cols 1 + 2)	Ideal Score	Improvement Opportunity (Cols 4 - 3)	Sales-person	Sales Manager	Combined Rating (Cols 6 + 7)	Ideal Score	Improvement Opportunity (Cols 9 - 8)	Actual Improvement (Cols 10 - 5)
a) Enjoys and seeks out competitive situations in business and in sports	0 1 2 3 4 5	0 1 2 3 4 5		10		0 1 2 3 4 5	0 1 2 3 4 5		10		
b) Takes pride in being a good competitor and loves the glory of winning	0 1 2 3 4 5	0 1 2 3 4 5		10		0 1 2 3 4 5	0 1 2 3 4 5		10		
c) Is eager to invest long hours in practice and coaching to increase chances to win	0 1 2 3 4 5	0 1 2 3 4 5		10		0 1 2 3 4 5	0 1 2 3 4 5		10		
d) Is not afraid of losing; is willing to take on calculated risks to win	0 1 2 3 4 5	0 1 2 3 4 5		10		0 1 2 3 4 5	0 1 2 3 4 5		10		
e)	0 1 2 3 4 5	0 1 2 3 4 5		10		0 1 2 3 4 5	0 1 2 3 4 5		10		
f)	0 1 2 3 4 5	0 1 2 3 4 5		10		0 1 2 3 4 5	0 1 2 3 4 5		10		
Total desire to win score:											

MOTIVATION REVIEW

	First Review					Second Review					
	1	2	3	4	5	6	7	8	9	10	11
5 Persistence and discipline	Sales-person	Sales Manager	Combined Rating (Cols 1 + 2)	Ideal Score	Improvement Opportunity (Cols 4 - 3)	Sales-person	Sales Manager	Combined Rating (Cols 6 + 7)	Ideal Score	Improvement Opportunity (Cols 9 - 8)	Actual Improvement (Cols 10 - 5)
a) Ability to stick with a task until it is completely finished	0 1 2 3 4 5	0 1 2 3 4 5		10		0 1 2 3 4 5	0 1 2 3 4 5		10		
b) Ability to press on in the face of tough obstacles and challenges	0 1 2 3 4 5	0 1 2 3 4 5		10		0 1 2 3 4 5	0 1 2 3 4 5		10		
c) Ability to maintain a cool and relaxed appearance in tough situations	0 1 2 3 4 5	0 1 2 3 4 5		10		0 1 2 3 4 5	0 1 2 3 4 5		10		
d) Ability to stick to long-term goals and turn dreams into reality	0 1 2 3 4 5	0 1 2 3 4 5		10		0 1 2 3 4 5	0 1 2 3 4 5		10		
e)	0 1 2 3 4 5	0 1 2 3 4 5		10		0 1 2 3 4 5	0 1 2 3 4 5		10		
f)	0 1 2 3 4 5	0 1 2 3 4 5		10		0 1 2 3 4 5	0 1 2 3 4 5		10		
Total persistance and descipline score:											

MOTIVATION REVIEW

	First Review					Second Review					
	1 Sales-person	**2** Sales Manager	**3** Combined Rating (Cols 1 + 2)	**4** Ideal Score	**5** Improvement Opportunity (Cols 4 - 3)	**6** Sales-person	**7** Sales Manager	**8** Combined Rating (Cols 6 + 7)	**9** Ideal Score	**10** Improvement Opportunity (Cols 9 - 8)	**11** Actual Improvement (Cols 10 - 5)
6 Handling rejection and failure											
a) Ability to see failure and rejection as stepping stones, not stumbling blocks	0 1 2 3 4 5	0 1 2 3 4 5		10		0 1 2 3 4 5	0 1 2 3 4 5		10		
b) Ability to recover from setbacks in a short period of time	0 1 2 3 4 5	0 1 2 3 4 5		10		0 1 2 3 4 5	0 1 2 3 4 5		10		
c) Ability to maintain hope during tough times and have faith in the recovery process	0 1 2 3 4 5	0 1 2 3 4 5		10		0 1 2 3 4 5	0 1 2 3 4 5		10		
d) Ability not to take failure and rejection too seriously and to maintain sense of humor	0 1 2 3 4 5	0 1 2 3 4 5		10		0 1 2 3 4 5	0 1 2 3 4 5		10		
e)	0 1 2 3 4 5	0 1 2 3 4 5		10		0 1 2 3 4 5	0 1 2 3 4 5		10		
f)	0 1 2 3 4 5	0 1 2 3 4 5		10		0 1 2 3 4 5	0 1 2 3 4 5		10		
Total handling rejection and failure score:											

MOTIVATION REVIEW

7 Managing disappointment

| | First Review ||||| Second Review ||||||
| | 1 | 2 | 3 | 4 | 5 | 6 | 7 | 8 | 9 | 10 | 11 |
	Sales-person	Sales Manager	Combined Rating (Cols 1 + 2)	Ideal Score	Improvement Opportunity (Cols 4 − 3)	Sales-person	Sales Manager	Combined Rating (Cols 6 + 7)	Ideal Score	Improvement Opportunity (Cols 9 − 8)	Actual Improvement (Cols 10 − 5)
a) Ability to maintain an active interest in a diverse number of activities besides work	0 1 2 3 4 5	0 1 2 3 4 5		10		0 1 2 3 4 5	0 1 2 3 4 5		10		
b) Ability to recognize disappointments as valuable personal growth experiences	0 1 2 3 4 5	0 1 2 3 4 5		10		0 1 2 3 4 5	0 1 2 3 4 5		10		
c) Ability to use disappointments to gain higher self-awareness and self-insight	0 1 2 3 4 5	0 1 2 3 4 5		10		0 1 2 3 4 5	0 1 2 3 4 5		10		
d) Ability to work through disappointments in a way that results in increased ambition	0 1 2 3 4 5	0 1 2 3 4 5		10		0 1 2 3 4 5	0 1 2 3 4 5		10		
e)	0 1 2 3 4 5	0 1 2 3 4 5		10		0 1 2 3 4 5	0 1 2 3 4 5		10		
f)	0 1 2 3 4 5	0 1 2 3 4 5		10		0 1 2 3 4 5	0 1 2 3 4 5		10		
Total disappointment management score:											

MOTIVATION REVIEW

	First Review					Second Review					
	1 Sales- person	**2** Sales Manager	**3** Combined Rating (Cols 1 + 2)	**4** Ideal Score	**5** Improvement Opportunity (Cols 4 − 3)	**6** Sales- person	**7** Sales Manager	**8** Combined Rating (Cols 6 + 7)	**9** Ideal Score	**10** Improvement Opportunity (Cols 9 − 8)	**11** Actual Improvement (Cols 10 − 5)
8 Positive living											
a) Ability to achieve a positive balance between work pressures and family demands	0 1 2 3 4 5	0 1 2 3 4 5		10		0 1 2 3 4 5	0 1 2 3 4 5		10		
b) Ability to maintain a healthy lifestyle that creates positive energy	0 1 2 3 4 5	0 1 2 3 4 5		10		0 1 2 3 4 5	0 1 2 3 4 5		10		
c) Ability to take time off for play, vacations, and/or community involvement	0 1 2 3 4 5	0 1 2 3 4 5		10		0 1 2 3 4 5	0 1 2 3 4 5		10		
d) Ability to experience joy, happiness, and fulfillment in life	0 1 2 3 4 5	0 1 2 3 4 5		10		0 1 2 3 4 5	0 1 2 3 4 5		10		
e)	0 1 2 3 4 5	0 1 2 3 4 5		10		0 1 2 3 4 5	0 1 2 3 4 5		10		
f)	0 1 2 3 4 5	0 1 2 3 4 5		10		0 1 2 3 4 5	0 1 2 3 4 5				
Total positive living score:											

MOTIVATION REVIEW

First Review | Second Review

9 Exercise and stress management	1 Sales-person	2 Sales Manager	3 Combined Rating (Cols 1 + 2)	4 Ideal Score	5 Improvement Opportunity (Cols 4 - 3)	6 Sales-person	7 Sales Manager	8 Combined Rating (Cols 6 + 7)	9 Ideal Score	10 Improvement Opportunity (Cols 9 - 8)	11 Actual Improvement (Cols 10 - 5)
a) Ability to stay with an aerobic exercise program on a regular basis	0 1 2 3 4 5	0 1 2 3 4 5		10		0 1 2 3 4 5	0 1 2 3 4 5		10		
b) Ability to practice healthy diet habits and maintain a healthy weight level	0 1 2 3 4 5	0 1 2 3 4 5		10		0 1 2 3 4 5	0 1 2 3 4 5		10		
c) Ability to cope with the daily stress of selling, mentally and physically	0 1 2 3 4 5	0 1 2 3 4 5		10		0 1 2 3 4 5	0 1 2 3 4 5		10		
d) Ability to maintain an optimistic outlook on life and find time for reflection	0 1 2 3 4 5	0 1 2 3 4 5		10		0 1 2 3 4 5	0 1 2 3 4 5		10		
e)	0 1 2 3 4 5	0 1 2 3 4 5		10		0 1 2 3 4 5	0 1 2 3 4 5		10		
f)	0 1 2 3 4 5	0 1 2 3 4 5		10		0 1 2 3 4 5	0 1 2 3 4 5		10		
Total exercise and stress management score:											

MOTIVATION REVIEW

10 Finding meaning and fulfillment

	First Review					Second Review					
	1 Sales-person	**2** Sales Manager	**3** Combined Rating (Cols 1 + 2)	**4** Ideal Score	**5** Improvement Opportunity (Cols 4 - 3)	**6** Sales-person	**7** Sales Manager	**8** Combined Rating (Cols 6 + 7)	**9** Ideal Score	**10** Improvement Opportunity (Cols 9 - 8)	**11** Actual Improvement (Cols 10 - 5)
a) Ability to view work, love, and play as key sources for meaning and fulfillment in life	0 1 2 3 4 5	0 1 2 3 4 5		10		0 1 2 3 4 5	0 1 2 3 4 5		10		
b) Ability to serve customers as a result of an inner need instead of external pressure	0 1 2 3 4 5	0 1 2 3 4 5		10		0 1 2 3 4 5	0 1 2 3 4 5		10		
c) Ability to pursue self-actualization as an achievable goal that deserves ongoing work	0 1 2 3 4 5	0 1 2 3 4 5		10		0 1 2 3 4 5	0 1 2 3 4 5		10		
d) Ability to commit to change with courage and to personal growth with guts	0 1 2 3 4 5	0 1 2 3 4 5		10		0 1 2 3 4 5	0 1 2 3 4 5		10		
e)	0 1 2 3 4 5	0 1 2 3 4 5		10		0 1 2 3 4 5	0 1 2 3 4 5		10		
f)	0 1 2 3 4 5	0 1 2 3 4 5		10		0 1 2 3 4 5	0 1 2 3 4 5				
Total meaning and fulfillment score:											

MOTIVATION REVIEW

First Review | Second Review

11 Additional category	1 Sales-person	2 Sales Manager	3 Combined Rating (Cols 1 + 2)	4 Ideal Score	5 Improvement Opportunity (Cols 4 − 3)	6 Sales-person	7 Sales Manager	8 Combined Rating (Cols 6 + 7)	9 Ideal Score	10 Improvement Opportunity (Cols 9 − 8)	11 Actual Improvement (Cols 10 − 5)
a)	0 1 2 3 4 5	0 1 2 3 4 5		10		0 1 2 3 4 5	0 1 2 3 4 5		10		
b)	0 1 2 3 4 5	0 1 2 3 4 5		10		0 1 2 3 4 5	0 1 2 3 4 5		10		
c)	0 1 2 3 4 5	0 1 2 3 4 5		10		0 1 2 3 4 5	0 1 2 3 4 5		10		
d)	0 1 2 3 4 5	0 1 2 3 4 5		10		0 1 2 3 4 5	0 1 2 3 4 5		10		
e)	0 1 2 3 4 5	0 1 2 3 4 5		10		0 1 2 3 4 5	0 1 2 3 4 5		10		
f)	0 1 2 3 4 5	0 1 2 3 4 5		10		0 1 2 3 4 5	0 1 2 3 4 5		10		
Total category score:											

Motivation Review Summary

	First Review	Second Review	Actual Improvement
Total salesperson score:			
Total sales manager score:			
Total combined rating:			
Total ideal score:			
Total improvement opportunity:			Improvement %

Motivation Improvement Plan

Please feel free to make a copy of this page for your salesperson.

Salesperson		Date
Areas to be improved	**Actions to be taken**	**By when**
1.		
2.		
3.		
4.		
5.		
6.		
7.		
8.		
9.		
10.		
11.		
12.		

Sales manager's signature   Salesperson's signature

Recommended Actions for Improving Sales Motivation

1. Reading Assignments

Here are a number of "must read" motivational books for your salespeople. Most of these can be purchased in paperback at your local bookstore:

The Power of Positive Thinking
by Dr. Norman Vincent Peale
See You At The Top
by Zig Ziglar
Think and Grow Rich
by Napolean Hill
The Sky is the Limit
by Dr. Wayne Dyer
The Psychology of Winning
by Dr. Denis Waitley
The Road Less Traveled
by Dr. Scott Peck
How to Win Friends and Influence People
by Dale Carnegie
How I Raised Myself From Failure to Success in Selling
by Frank Bettger
Maximum Achievement
by Brian Tracy
Feeling Good
by Dr. David Burns
Overcoming Procrastination
by Dr. Albert Ellis
The Courage to Fail
by Art Mortell

In addition, the following Essential Readings in Part Two will provide individuals on your sales team more resources for boosting their motivation.

- Ethics in Thought and Action
- Being a Professional in Every Way
- Working with Your Boss
- Keys to Self-Improvement
- Stress-Reduction Basics
- Always Strive for Success

2. Motivational Speakers

Here are some of the top motivational speakers to address your salespeople:

Zig Ziglar
Dr. Denis Waitley
Dr. Wayne Dyer
Anthony Robbins
Terry Bradshaw
Norman Schwarzkopf
Scott Kramnick
Brian Tracy
Mary Lou Retton
Lou Holtz
Art Mortell
Tom Hopkins
Fran Tarkenton
Pat Riley
Don Hutson

3. Personal Coaching

Salespeople who need a change in attitude can often benefit greatly by working with several of the top people on out sales team. Greatness breeds greatness. If you expose your average salesperson to the top talents in your company, you will soon notice a significant change in motivation and sales results.

4. Create Rewards that Motivate

Salespeople love opportunities to win. Create a meaningful incentive program that recognizes salespeople for their extra efforts. Salespeople go the extra mile—providing you give them the extra recognition they need. A handshake from the company president at the podium in front of the entire sales staff and a thoughtful incentive award is remembered longer than a bonus check hidden in an envelope.

5. The Sales Manager as Motivator

Remember that for every action, there is an equal and opposite reaction. Attitude begets attitude. If you treat your salespeople as special individuals, they will treat you as a special sales manager.

A genuine smile, a pat on the back, a handwritten note that says "thank you" for a job a well done can work wonders. Write brief, but highly personal notes to your salespeople. Mary Kay Ash sent tens of thousands of personal notes to her sales staff and developed one of the greatest sales organizations in the country.

Below is s select listing of a few companies that specialize in printing "Thank You" notes and creative greeting cards that salespeople and customers will enjoy receiving. Call these companies for a free catalog:

Harrison Publishing Company
Asheville, NC (800) 438-5829
Posty Cards
Kansas City, MO (816) 231-2323
IntroKnocks
New York, NY (800) 753-0590

Motivation Improvement Checklist

Complete this form three months after your initial review meeting.

1. Did salesperson complete the action plan 100 percent?
   ❑ Yes
   ❑ No
2. If you answered "No" to the above question, indicate reasons for not completing the action plan:

_____

_____

3. Did salesperson complete the action plan on time?
   ❑ Yes
   ❑ No
4. What was the total improvement opportunity? _____
5. What was the actual improvement score? _____
6. What was the improvement percentage? _____

To calculate the improvement percentage, multiply the actual improvement score (Column 11) by 100 and divide by the total improvement opportunity (Column 5). Ex: $20 \times 100 = 2000 \div 40 = 50\%$

7. If the improvement percentage is 5 percent or higher, enter the improvement percentage in the appropriate space of the sales improvement certificate at the end of this book.

How to Calculate and Use Your Team Score

To determine the percentage increase of the motivation of your team, use the Sales Team Performance Summary in the pages that follow. The five steps below are guidelines to user as you assess the team.

1. Add up each salesperson's score and add up your total team score.
2. Note the differences in motivation within your sales team. Try to have those salespeople with high scores help those with the lowest scores.
3. Set a motivation improvement goal for your entire sales team.
4. Measure your progress after three months. Compare the new score with the old score and determine your team improvement percentage.
5. Create a special group incentive to reward improved performance.

Sales Team Performance Summary Motivation: First Review

Please transcribe the improvement opportunity scores (Column 5) of all your salespeople onto this page. Date: _____

Name of Salesperson:											
1. Positive thinking											
2. Enthusiasm											
3. Self-confidence											
4. Desire to win											
5. Persistence and discipline											
6. Handling rejection and failure											
7. Managing disappointment											
8. Positive living											
9. Exercise and stress management											
10. Finding meaning and fulfillment											
11.											
Total sales team score—Motivation:											

Sales Team Performance Summary Motivation: Second Review

Please transcribe the improvement opportunity scores (Column 5) of all your salespeople onto this page.   Date: _____

Name of Salesperson:											
1. Positive thinking											
2. Enthusiasm											
3. Self-confidence											
4. Desire to win											
5. Persistence and discipline											
6. Handling rejection and failure											
7. Managing disappointment											
8. Positive living											
9. Exercise and stress management											
10. Finding meaning and fulfillment											
11.											
Total sales team score—Motivation:											

PART TWO

Essential Readings for Individual Growth

Essential Readings About Knowledge

CHAPTER FIVE
Getting Past Gatekeepers

Cracking the Vault

How to Make Allies of Executive Assistants Who Can Get You Through to Top Decision Makers

It may seem like a mystery, but in reality it's plain-old common sense why some people who call the CEO of a company get to hear the golden words—"Just a minute please while I put you through"—whereas others get a click as the line goes dead. The simple truth is, doing your homework and maintaining a respectful manner are still what counts when it comes to making a meaningful connection with an executive assistant who closely guards the boss's time.

"Salespeople have a one-minute window for me to decide," says Joan Avagliano, executive assistant to Robert Dilenschneider, who heads The Dilenschneider Group, a globally known public relations and marketing company. "Knowing whom you're calling, having the right information in front of you, and having a service we really need are key," she notes. Salespeople who have the right information help her decide whether to pass the call on to her boss or ask for more information that could lead to a sale further down the road.

Like many gatekeepers, Avagliano tries to be mindful of the person on the other end of the phone line. "I'm very gracious to salespeople, because they have a tough job," she says. "But if they have Mr. Dilenschneider's name wrong, I'm much tougher on them." Common tip-offs that a caller is unfamiliar with the company include requests to speak with Dillon, Robert (he prefers Bob), or Mr. Schneider. Even so, Avagliano tries to be careful about making assumptions because, as she puts it, "you never know."

Patience, however, is a requirement for both caller and assistant. "When you're trying to sell something, and I say, 'Thank you, I haven't made a decision about it,' I mean it. There are some days when I can't listen to a spiel. If I say that I'll call you back, I will," says Avagliano, who tries to be very up-front in her dealings. She admires persistence, and when she asks a salesperson to check in every quarter, and they do, she is much more inclined to throw business their way.

In addition to having salespeople take their cues from her, Avagliano is careful about listening to what they say. Buzzwords such as "cost-cutting"—which led to the company's current phone system (sold by a cold caller)—make her take note. If Avagliano has a complaint, it's when salespeople try to make an end-run around her entirely and tell her that a call is personal. "I've worked with Mr. Dilenschneider for 18 years," she says, "and I know."

Similarly, at SAP America Inc., the U.S. arm of the German enterprise software maker SAP AG, Barbara Rendina, executive assistant to president and CEO Bill McDermott, also tries to treat each caller with respect. "You always have to be responsive, because you never know who's on the other end. Even the calls you get at home at night are from people just doing their jobs. A huge part of my job as Bill's assistant is to be an extension of him. He's extremely responsive and respectful." Her number-one piece of advice for cold callers is to "be really prepared. Say who you are, why you're calling, and why you specifically need to talk to Bill. A lot of times I'll ask them to put it in an e-mail. We have a great network of internal people; it doesn't always have to go through Bill."

Even though Rendina checks her BlackBerry at night and early in the morning, she still prefers to begin a relationship with a call. "Probably what works best is to phone and introduce yourself and then follow up with e-mail," she says. Of course, with so many viruses, she prefers not to open e-mails from people she doesn't know.

"How many salespeople blow a relationship before they ever get to the decision maker?" asks Kevin Malmos, general manager at InfoUSA, which maintains one of the largest databases of businesses and consumers under one roof. As part of his job, heading up a unit of 20 to 25 people responsible for 100,000 phone calls a month, he works to prevent just that. For Malmos, the key element that salespeople too often overlook is "respecting the executive assistant as a major player, and not looking at that person as a hurdle. Salespeople have to realize that person is a key to your success." He encourages salespeople to cultivate assistants, and other "alternative contacts," such as members of IT staff. "Use that person not only to find out information," he advises, "but to help with the decision-making."

To borrow from Humphrey Bogart in *Casablanca*, salespeople who do their due diligence before talking with an executive assistant—and follow through—just might find that this is the start of a beautiful [business] relationship.

Tips for Going Around and Through Sales Barricades

If salespeople were in charge, the term *voice mail* would probably officially be changed to "(expletive deleted) voice mail." And if you want to keep the conversation friendly, don't even bring up the topic of gatekeepers with a group of salespeople. But according to Art Sobczak, the uncrowned king of telephone selling, there are ways around and through these formidable selling obstacles.

1. *Where are you going?* When a screener isn't sure what to do about your call, don't just let him pass you off onto someone else. Before you are connected to the next unwitting person, find out that individual's name and title.
2. *Push up.* Always seek the level above where buying decisions are typically made. So when you're referred, say "I was speaking with Alan in Mr. Donovan's office and he felt that Ms. Ferguson is the person I should speak with." When your call is coming from a high level, it carries more weight.
3. *Bounce around.* Let screeners send you to other peripheral departments. Gather knowledge wherever you can, whether it's in purchasing or even sales. Try saying "Can you help me? I'm not in the right department, but you can probably give me some direction. I'm Sue Jones with Dirigible Package Express. I'm looking for the person who handles shipping decisions in your organization."
4. *Prepare for the beep.* Always be ready to get voice mail. In your message, talk briefly about ideas you have that can benefit the customer, then say you'd like to ask a few follow-up questions to determine what will work for them.
5. *Turn on the charm.* Just because you're talking to a machine doesn't mean you have to sound like one, too. Be yourself. Consider the person who will later listen to the message. Tape record yourself and practice your inflection and conveying moods like enthusiasm, urgency, and importance. And remember to articulate—don't mumble!

Creative Ways for Tackling Any Block

With the proliferation of voice mail, administrative assistants and all other varieties of obstacles placed in your path, today's typical buyer is about as accessible as the South Pole in the middle of a blizzard. But with a little ingenuity, sales professionals like Ohio-based lumber representative Mike Stieritz have developed methods to bypass the blocks and win those critical one-on-one presentations. Following are Stieritz's six top tips for breaking through to the other side:

1. *He who is without sincere....* When leaving voice mail, be enthusiastic, sincere and offer a compelling reason for customers to call you back. Mention a reason, any reason—a new product release, for example—then promise to be brief when prospects call you back. And if they do call, make good on the promise.
2. *Humor them.* Humor works to bring recalcitrant prospects around. If you've left several messages with no response, jokingly ask if you've done something to make them angry. Make prospects laugh and you'll stand out from the crowd.
3. *Make an ally.* If you keep reaching assistants, get their names. Then say, "I know [the boss] is very busy, but I promise to be brief and not waste time if you can help get [the boss] to call me back or if you can find the best time for me to call." If you're friendly and engaging, assistants will be much more willing to help you.
4. *Keep an ally.* If an assistant does help you to get through, call back or send a note of thanks expressing your appreciation. Very few people do this, but it goes a long way. The next time you go in or call, that person is going to remember you.

5. *Get personal.* Try to personalize your mail or fax messages. If you get gatekeepers, try to find out something specific about the prospects that you can use. Then, if you find out anything—like the day they play golf in the afternoon or that their division has just finished a record-setting quarter—use that information to personalize your message.
6. *Don't have a cow; have a purpose.* Have a purpose for every phone call. Before you pick up the phone, ask yourself, "What do I want to accomplish?" Then be ready for that voice mail. Have something ready that will sound enticing. Too many salespeople say, "I just want to touch base with you." That's too general—prospects don't have time to chat and won't bother to return your call.

CHAPTER SIX
Generating Leads

Get Involved!

Developing and cultivating leads should be a continual, fundamental part of every business. Don't give up when the going is good; constantly seek new ways to expand your center of influence, says Kristin Woods, author of *Sales Source* and a territory manager for State Auto.

"Participate in any associations or groups that your customers or prospects are involved in, so that your center of influence is always expanding. By your interacting with them in a professional or personal affiliation, they serve as a visual referral—you're connected to them. When they introduce you, they can introduce you through their relationship with you. For example, 'This is Kris Woods. Kris handles my insurance. We've worked together for a number of years. If you have insurance concerns, I feel very comfortable with Kris.'

"Get involved in organizations and nonprofits. But be prepared to give before you can expect to take. Donate time, money, or some sort of resource so that the group can benefit. This can be a natural flow to bring business back to you—but don't just join the group and sit back.

"If you come through for a committee or in a group, the message you send to prospects is 'She delivered on that fund-raising committee, so she'll probably deliver in business.'"

Joining groups, coaching, or joining a country club all boils down to one thing: a common bond with your prospect or customer. And who knows where that may lead you?

Buyer Be Where?

Anyone who's played three-card Monte knows what it's like trying to track down a decision maker in some customer organizations. Just when you think you're on the right track, the cards are reshuffled and the ace of spades eludes you. Steve Grandinetti, a sales manager with Iowa-based Mill-Tech, a mill reengineering firm, believes that there are two reasons why today's decision makers have become so scarce.

"Most companies today are so downsized that the people in purchasing don't know enough about what they're doing to make a decision," Grandinetti argues. "All they can do is ask for a quote and then bring it to their boss for a decision. Second, a smaller-ticket item—which for us might be a $5,000 to $6,000 mill realignment—a shop supervisor or foreman will have the budget for that. But if we do a complete rebuild, that's more like $75,000 to $150,000, and that's when a comptroller or VP comes in saying, 'What are the benefits here?'"

For those big-ticket items, Grandinetti says that after dotting all his I's and crossing all his T's—working with a shop foreman to evaluate all the technical information and compile a competitive bid—his strategy is to call in some big guns of his own.

"We'll say, 'This is going to take a visit from our boss, the VP, maybe the director of operations,'" he says.

"So we'll plan that visit into our bid, going in and asking, 'Who's making this decision? Can we get in to see them? Can we have a meeting before you make a decision?' We try to ask that as we go along, then we're ahead of the game already."

Despite these efforts, Grandinetti acknowledges that his success rate drops precipitously whenever decisions get kicked upstairs. As a result, he concedes, sometimes he'll downgrade his expectations and try to pluck the lower-hanging fruit.

"If I can keep the dollar amounts between $25,000 and $50,000, I'm usually much better off," he says. "But each situation is different and has to be evaluated individually. The figure for some mills may be only $20,000. But the point is that sometimes it's better to go for the smaller amounts where I know I can talk to the decision maker on the factory floor and not have to depend on some bean counter back at corporate headquarters to look over the proposal. These are the bread-and-butter deals that keep the dollars rolling and the company running."

Seven Steps to More Sales Leads

1. **Research your market** Use directories or databases to uncover potential prospects. Look at company records to find old clients and rekindle relationships with them.
2. **Continuously seek referrals** Ask everyone you know for referrals, whether you're doing business with them or not.
3. **Be alert** Leads are all around you. Keep your eyes and ears open. Talk to people, even if they don't seem, on the surface at least, to be likely prospects.

4. **Attend or exhibit at trade shows** The attendees are already somewhat qualified by the nature of the show.
5. **Network and build relationships** with other people in your industry and professionals in other arenas.
6. **Calculate what you're willing to pay for a lead.** Leave no stone unturned. Test such different promotions and media as direct mail and trade or consumer advertising. You never know until you try.
7. **Cold call** Remember that each "no" you receive takes you one step closer to a "yes."

CHAPTER SEVEN
Perfecting Product Knowledge

Keys for Selling New Products

When promoting a new product, choreography is everything—from coordinating the product's introduction to coincide with the marketing blitz to ramping up the sales reps' training just as customers begin to ask "Hey, when's the new model coming out?" This Essential Reading features sound advice on making your next new product rollout a *tour de force* performance from two reps who are masters of learning about their products: Nancy Miles, a sales manager with the Power Tool Company in Johnson City, Tennessee, and Randy Scott, a sales engineer for Square D in Altamonte Springs, Florida.

According to Scott, who sells the Grainger line of electronic products to Square D's channel partners, salespeople can only sell new products effectively if they have adequate notice about what's coming down the pike and receive the appropriate training on the new products.

"It's all about awareness and education," he says. "We can come out with a new product and just put it out there, but unless we're educated on that product beforehand, it's going to be difficult for us. That's because the customer's going to come back to the sales rep with all sorts of questions and objections, and we have to be prepared for that.

"For example, we're coming out with a new plastic disconnect soon. It's being introduced very shortly, and I didn't even know it was coming out. It's exciting that we're going to get it, but I'd like some advance notice so that I can do the necessary preparation."

Miles views the same challenge from a management perspective. With her field reps, who sell the company's lawn maintenance machines from dispersed locations, the problem with training is geographical.

"Our reps are always very knowledgeable and enthusiastic about new products," she says. "But sometimes it's a logistical challenge sharing product information with them. We either have to bring them in to where we are or we'll all go to the manufacturer who is producing the new products so we can get up to speed in a hurry. It's not an insurmountable challenge, but it does mean they have to take time away from making sales calls."

It's one thing to generate excitement about a new product with the company's salespeople; it's a greater challenge to breed that same enthusiasm among customers. The best way to start, says Scott, is to involve your customers ahead of time, during the product development stage.

"You hope your new products are going to meet a bunch of the customer's needs," he says. "As the manufacturer, we assess those needs and design the product accordingly. Of course it helps if you're in contact with customers about these issues, but it's even better if they can have direct input, to get from the horse's mouth, so to speak, what the crucial issues are. That way, during the design stage you can either enhance the product accordingly or take out something that's not important."

Once the product has been developed, however, both Scott and Miles agree that new-product selling requires an effort keyed directly to meeting specific customer needs that will justify taking a chance on an unproven commodity.

"Certainly, the product has to solve a problem for the customer," Scott notes. "With our customers that means either reducing or removing costs. Distributors want to keep their inventory at a low cost. When we come out with something new, they're hesitant to put it out without any proven wins for them. So first, it has to be a problem solver—it has to address a concern they have about the existing product. Second, we need to demo it for them, show how it will work. Third, we have to leave samples with them. Fourth, and this actually takes place before the other three, we have to plant the seed of enthusiasm for the product in the customer's mind ahead of time. That way once we do have it in our hands, half the selling job is already done."

Miles echoes these sentiments, emphasizing that in the power tool business, the challenge lies in persuading customers to open up floor space for untested new products. "We have to demonstrate two things to our customers, who may be mom-and-pop stores or national chains like Ace Hardware," she explains. "One, they want to know 'How is this product going to add to my product line?' Then second, 'How's it going to benefit my customers?' We've got to show them the benefits as well as the need in the market. There has to be a niche in the market we're exploiting or they're not going to want to part with that valuable floor space.

"These are big pieces of equipment, not something that sits on a shelf. And a lot of times customers will say, 'If someone comes in and asks for it, I'll sell it to them.' But a customer may not even know that it exists unless they can see it, feel it, and demo it."

The best way to accomplish this, Miles emphasizes, is by tying the new solution to concerns the customer is sure to recognize.

"With a new and improved version, there's also probably an additional cost. But you have to go beyond just saying 'new and improved' over and over again like a TV commercial. You have to show them the increased productivity or how it's going to cause less fatigue for the machine's operator. Or a lot of times what has changed on these products is something that has caused them problems in the shop with maintenance. So if the improvement is a better clutch or a difference in the way the operator changes the level of the mowing deck, that's a change that will have meaning for them. And those are the hot buttons you have to key on."

Scott is equally hot on hot buttons. For your new products, which you hope will help customers solve the problems of tomorrow, he believes the salesperson should capitalize on growing industry trends on both the sales and marketing sides.

"Besides just talking about features and benefits, you have to show how the product is current," he explains. "In our industry, a very hot term right now is 'energy savings.' That's what gets customers' attention and that's what everyone is focusing on right now. So with new products especially, we have to highlight energy savings. Because even if the product has a lot of great benefits, energy savings is what's going to make the customer sit up and take notice.

"And the same holds true for the peripheral tools you use. Sure, you can do a mass mailing like you've always done in the past, but today it's probably better to use the power of the Internet. Put something on your company Web site and send customers the address. Then they can go look at it and invest a little of their time to get acquainted with what's up and coming. That investment will pay dividends down the line when the product arrives and the customer says, 'Oh yeah, I was wondering when I would get my hands on one of these.'"

CHAPTER EIGHT
Outselling Your Competition

Outselling Your Competition

The largest sale Mark Meyer ever landed was with a company that was close to making a decision to go with another service. "This company had hired a third-party consultant who had an allegiance to our competitor," says Meyer, a regional sales manager in the New York area for UpShot Corporation. The consultant called Meyer and asked for some pricing information.

That seemingly innocuous information call was key to the entire sale. Why? Because Meyer was paying attention. He was reading between the lines. "That call gave me the heads-up. I thought, 'This company—a potentially huge account—is in the market for a CRM service.'"

It took some doing on Meyer's part, but after two weeks of phone calling he got a meeting with the company. "Once they saw what we could do for them, they signed with us."

Meyer believes that finding out your potential clients are planning to buy from the competition is not necessarily bad news. "If they're speaking with your competitors, at least you know they are interested in what you have to sell." And that is an excellent place to start.

"The first step when dealing with purchasing managers who buy from the competition," says Tim McCormack of Ace World Wide Moving, "is to get them to open their minds to a new company."

The first phone contact is critical. "You have to get a meeting," says McCormack. "When we make the call, we say we just want to ask them a few questions about their current situation." If they ask what those questions are, don't tell them over the phone, says McCormack. "Wait till you have them in front of you."

What do you say in that first phone call? "Don't start on a hard-sell. Don't go off on how great your company is," McCormack advises. "Tell them you know their time is valuable, but you would like to have just 30 minutes of it just to see if there is anything you could do for them."

If that doesn't work, McCormack suggests asking, "If there was one thing I could do to prove that I was worth 30 minutes of your time, what would that be?"

When you do get that first meeting, Meyer suggests you ask a few key questions: Why did you subscribe or buy from that company? What were you expecting? Did you get it? What do you like about it? What do you still wish for?

"Something usually gets missed," explains Meyer, who believes that follow-up is a key part of sales and is often overlooked. "Competitors often promise a lot and then may not deliver."

Research is also a large part of that first sales meeting. "We literally study the psychology of the company and the potential buyer," says McCormack. "We look at the history of the company's sales and purchasing, at the company's business and employee profile. If you go in informed, with ideas about how this particular company could improve its performance if it used your product, you are going in client focused and you could very well land the sale."

But what happens if you don't land the sale or, even worse, you failed to get that first face-to-face meeting? "It's not the end of the world," says McCormack. "You have to think long-term." After that first meeting, whether the clients say "yes," "no thank you," or "maybe later," McCormack keeps in touch with them.

"If we fail to get to where we want to be on the first meeting or first contact, we put them into our database. We look at them as future clients, and we begin what we call our 'Touch Campaign.'"

UpShot assigns every client and potential client to a sales team that supports their reps through research, strategizing, and organizing future sales. "We look at how we could improve their lives and their work. We may send an article about our company or a piece that relates to their company and their needs. Sending information that shows we understand their business and their needs says, 'We're here to help.' It's the best way to turn a potential client into a current buyer."

CHAPTER NINE
Dealing with Difficult Customers

How to Turn Around Difficult Customers—and Yourself

If you had to pick which of Snow White's diminutive companions best represents your most difficult customers, which would it be? Bashful? Dopey? Grumpy? The little-known eighth dwarf, "Can't Decide?" Unfortunately, there's little you can do directly to change your customers' attitudes. But, authors Stacey Hall and Jan Brogniez say, we can change our approach to those around us, and just maybe help some of those Grumpys find their inner Happys. In *Attracting Perfect Customers: The Power of Strategic Synchronicity*, Hall and Brogniez recommend the following eight-step approach:

1. Think about a situation from the past week when a customer's behavior irritated or frustrated you.
2. Recall what the customer did that you found objectionable. Was he or she rude, late, hostile, or dishonest?

3. On a piece of paper, make a list of everything about the behavior that bothered you.
4. Next to each negative behavior, write the opposite attitude you'd prefer to see from that person. Next to "dishonest," for example, you might write "open," "truthful," "straightforward," and so forth. Follow suit for each negative behavior on your list.
5. Take another look at the original list of negative qualities.
6. Think about whether you have recently demonstrated any of these negative qualities yourself. Have you been less than forthcoming with anyone (your boss, the IRS, a customer, your spouse, etc.) in the past week?
7. Write down how you'd prefer to act the next time such a situation arises.
8. Let yourself and the other person you've used for this example off the hook. Rather than beating yourself up or holding a grudge against the customer, take a fresh tack. Resolve to improve your relationship—both with yourself and with customers who tend to get your dander up.

Powerful Tips to Disarm Toxic Remarks

So what do you do if your client is acting like your meetings are a big hassle, making remarks under his breath? or is constantly putting you on the defensive by making negative comments about your service? How do you respond without escalating these situations? Joyce Weiss gives some powerful tips for disarming toxic comments in her *Take the Ride of Your Life*.

1. *Use verbal aikido,* which means that you diffuse pessimism and create optimism by accepting, redirecting, and reaffirming, says Weiss. "The cardinal rule of verbal aikido is to not repeat

the accusation," explains Weiss. "For example, someone asks: Why are you wasting my money? Don't say: We're not wasting your money. Instead, respond: Let me tell you what we are doing with your money. This response gives the person nothing to push against. Verbal aikido is a skill that gives you back the control. It helps you focus on what can be done."
2. *Try empathy.* "Ask yourself: How would I feel if I were in that person's shoes?" says Weiss. "Try to figure out why that person is behaving this way. Doing so will help you respond, not react." Could it be the person has had a bad experience previously? Once you understand what's going on, you might be able to present your ideas differently.
3. *Be accountable.* "Don't explain or defend yourself when something goes wrong," says Weiss. "Explanations come across as excuses. Agree, if what is being said is true. Acknowledge, apologize, and act."

For example, a customer screams at you because she didn't receive her product on time. Even if it wasn't your fault, don't try and push the blame. Simply, say: You're right. It is late and I'm sorry. I'll get it to you today. This technique, says Weiss, gives you what she calls prepared flexibility or the ability to roll with the punches.

Using Nonverbal Skills to Build Strong Customer Relationships

1. Look to the client for cues on how much time to spend socializing at the beginning of a sales call. In the early stages of a client relationship, a minute or two should suffice.
2. Come up with a few provocative questions that will help you understand your clients as people.

> 3. Look around the clients' offices for clues to their interests. Use them as conversational openers and as insight into how they like to conduct business.
> 4. Try to connect with what the client is feeling. When you begin to feel a genuine empathy with that person, your empathy will be transmitted through eye contact.
> 5. Segue to the meat of the meeting with an agenda-setting statement that recaps who you are, what company you represent, and the purpose of the meeting.

Dale Carnegie's Strategies for Winning Friends

Dale Carnegie died long ago, but the techniques he laid out in his classic book *How to Win Friends and Influence People* continue to resonate today. Use the following tips to take a page out of this bestseller and paste it into your own selling efforts:

1. Carnegie wrote, "If you want to persuade someone to your point of view, make him feel like somebody." Prospects and customers will appreciate you much more if you show a genuine interest in their thoughts and opinions. Treat them like the valued experts they are and they'll be much more willing to share the information that will help you sell to them more effectively.
2. Carnegie firmly believed in the power of failure, but only if you are wise enough to use the lessons of failure to improve for the future. When you do not succeed—lost sale, missed opportunity, and so forth—rather than getting upset at yourself or trying to pretend it didn't happen, retrace your steps in search of the seeds of the failure. What could you have done differently

(or more importantly, what can you do differently in the future) to avoid failure?
3. Put the power of yes to work for you. Carnegie taught that by getting people to agree with you on a series of smaller points, you improve your chances of hearing that most important yes—when you ask for the order.

Another Carnegie *bon mot* was "The only way to get the best of an argument is to avoid it." Argue with your customers and you may win the debate, but you'll almost certainly lose the sale. Instead of confronting differences of opinion head on, try a more circuitous route by saying things like, "Let me show you why I feel the way I do" or "I understand your viewpoint. Here's another perspective I've found valuable."

Elevate Your Value in Customers' Eyes

Which sounds more enticing: (a) buying a product from a sales rep or (b) entering into a partnership with a recognized expert in the field? If you answered "a," put on that cone-shaped hat and sit in the corner. You are the weakest link. But your customers know the score. They want to feel confident about their buying decisions and that they're acting based on the best information available. So how do you position yourself as an industry expert? In *Close More Sales! Persuasion Techniques That Boost Your Selling Power*, author Mike Stewart suggests the following nine tips:

1. *Study.* Become a student of your business, your industry, your own company, its products and the trends that will likely affect you, your customers, and the industry as a whole.
2. *Be certifiable.* What certification designations does your industry offer? Participate in local associations, serve on

committees, and seek positions of leadership and visibility wherever possible within your industry.

3. *Take notes.* Unless you're blessed with a photographic memory, then facts, figures, and dates will escape your long-term memory. But they can't escape a notebook or journal you keep handy for writing down such pieces of information that you can use later.
4. *Sound like an expert.* Instead of saying to customers, "I think that," or, "I guess," say, "In my experience," or, "In my professional opinion...."
5. *Cite sources.* Unless you made it up, explain where you got your information. "In the *Wall Street Journal* yesterday...," "According to your company's latest annual report...," "In Tom Peters' new book...."
6. *Tell and show.* If you've got the article, book, or report handy, fork it over. This will impress upon the customer that you are, in fact, an expert and well versed in all aspects of the industry.
7. *Write stuff.* If you have a particularly salient point you want to get across, write it down, whether on a dry-erase board, an overhead, or just on a sheet of paper. Visuals have a powerful impact that customers feel.
8. *Give 'em the fingers.* If you have three points to make, hold up three fingers and tick off the points one by one.
9. *Give more than a token gesture.* Your gestures should be rehearsed enough to come naturally to you but not so studied as to appear stilted. Mere words can only accomplish so much, but the right gesture can help drive a point home.

CHAPTER TEN
Win–Win Negotiations

How to Use Negotiation to Increase Sales

Just about everything in life is negotiable. You negotiate daily with your family, co-workers, and boss. Sometimes you even negotiate with yourself. Should I do this, or should I do that? You may not realize it, but negotiating is part of daily life.

Negotiating a sale with a prospect or current customer is similar, but more focused. Here are some expert tips on how to improve your negotiating skills.

- *Go for the win–win situation.* It takes two to tango, and while you want to walk out of your clients' doors with a sale, they also need to feel that they've benefited and won from the transaction. You're future business depends on it.
- *Do your research.* Negotiate from a position of power. That means having as much information on your prospect as you can. As the Boy Scouts say, "Be prepared."
- *Set your goals for the negotiations.* Develop strategies, tactics, and counteractions. Be proactive and anticipate what your

counterparts want and need and the direction in which they might go.
- *Let your counterparts speak first while you listen*—with undivided attention, no interruptions, and an open mind. Don't listen to respond.
- *When you ask questions, ask good ones.* Like Sherlock Holmes, your business is to gain information and "know what other people don't know."
- *Read nonverbal communications.* Keep your eyes focused on your counterparts and their gestures and body language. How they physically react, or don't react, is sometimes more important than what they say.
- *Don't give up the farm.* Your goal is a win–win outcome: you don't want to be on the short end of the stick. Remember, you can always walk away.

Overcoming the Eight Biggest Negotiating Mistakes

Although we all go into negotiations determined to come out on top, we often give away more than necessary to close the sale.

It may be easy to jump into the negotiating arena, but winning at the game is another matter. Your effectiveness will increase dramatically if you become aware of the most common negotiating mistakes and then learn how to avoid them.

Mistake No. 1: Underestimating Your Power

When you want someone to buy your product, it is natural to feel anxious. Before you realize it, you may become preoccupied with how important the sale is to you, both for your ego and for your income. Although there is nothing wrong with looking at the situation from your own point of view, you may lose perspective.

In negotiating, your strength and power lie in focusing on what you can do for your customer, not on what your customer can do for you. Keep in mind that your product is going to solve some very serious problems for your customer. To negotiate from a position of power, you must sincerely believe that doing business with you is a plus for the customer.

Mistake No. 2: Negotiating Without the Final Decision Maker

Even seasoned professionals sometimes fail to make sure they are negotiating with the final fund releaser. This is not to say that you foolishly forgot to ask, "Can you make the final purchasing decision?" Very often the answer to this question is "Yes." When the crunch comes, however, a mysterious committee that has to give final approval suddenly surfaces. The trap is that you are pushed to give your best and final price, only to find out that the committee has to approve. The committee, not surprisingly, wants you to offer a better deal again. Now it's back to the concessions board.

To get around this set up, pin down all decision makers: "Is there anyone, aside from yourself, who will be involved in making the final decision?" Also establish the rules for negotiating. Ask, "If we worked out an agreement that is comfortable for you, would you be prepared to complete the paperwork today?" These questions will force out the true situation. If you find that a committee must approve, push to attend the committee meeting yourself. If this is not acceptable, you have two choices: either put in your price/term package and leave yourself room to negotiate, or give them your best package and make it clear that you will not make any changes. If you take the second course, stick to what you have said.

Mistake No. 3: Thinking About Your Price in a Vacuum

Because it's the fastest, most effective way to get you to lower your price, customers will usually tell you that your price is too high. Because it works, they reason, why not continue to use it?

Price is always too high if the purchaser is not getting anything back for the money spent. If I said, "I am asking $5,000 for a stone I am selling," you would probably say that I was crazy. But if the stone was a one-carat unblemished diamond, you might grab at the opportunity to turn a profit. The mistake is in thinking about price in a vacuum.

Always talk about price in relation to the value purchased by the money being spent. Will the purchase increase productivity, improve ease of daily operations, increase sales, reduce expenses, or increase the bottom line in some other way? Then when your customer talks about the price being too high, you can talk about how the expenditure will be recovered or what benefits that purchase will bring to your customer's company.

Mistake No. 4: Forgetting to Justify Your Price

If we were not slaves to our emotions, it would appear quite logical to explain the rationale for our prices again rather than quickly reducing the price. After all, when your customer says that your price is too high, he means that he does not appreciate the value of your product. At this point, before you even consider reducing your price, you must review the benefits that your product will provide and the price tag attached to the opportunity to enjoy these benefits.

Mistake No. 5: Lowering Your Price Too Quickly

To negotiate without dropping your price, you can extend your service contract a couple of months, offer some consultation time to solve a particular problem, provide a free maintenance check, or do a small piece of additional work at no extra charge; or, throw in a couple of additional concessions on your company's part: add 30 days to the terms of payment, improve speed of delivery, or provide product storage. If you can tie it into a problem that your customer needs to solve, whatever you offer will be extremely effective.

Mistake No. 6: Negotiating Your Price Too Soon

Your customer says, "Your price is too high." You respond with, "Well, how would a 2 percent discount sound to you?" You drop your price immediately. In doing so, you probably don't realize how you have weakened your selling position. Your action says, "This product really isn't worth very much in itself. It is only worth what you will pay for it. So why don't we agree on what you want to pay for it, and as long as you are reasonable, we can make a deal." In the end, your customer may lose trust in you for attempting to rip him off with your (initially) high price.

When your customer first requests a price reduction, ask, "What makes you feel that the price is too high?" Let your customer put forth his or her argument for why you should accept the price reduction request. Insist upon a reason.

Mistake No. 7: Reducing Your Price Without Asking for a Return Concession

When you do make a price concession, be sure to ask for a concession from your customer in return. "If you give in to a price negotiation once, why shouldn't you give in again?" your customer reasons. On the other hand, if you ask for a concession from your customer, he will think twice about continuing the negotiation game. It is not as rewarding if he has to give up something, too.

In exchange for a price reduction, you might ask your customer to purchase additional quantities of the same product, or some related add-on product. You can ask your customer to extend his service contract with you for three to six additional months, request shorter terms of payment, offer fewer features, vary the delivery schedule, or reduce the product quality.

Mistake No. 8: Forgetting That You Are Giving Away Your Company's Profits

Negotiations can become so all-consuming that you can lose the big picture. Every dollar that you negotiate away comes off your company's profits and your own sales commission.

To stay on top of profits, watch the zeros. Don't negotiate in round numbers. Never offer a 1 or a 2 percent discount. Always connect your price concessions to actual reductions made on parts of the deal. For example, if your total package is $62,535 to include product and service, cut it down slowly by saying, "Well, maybe we can cut down on the second service call and charge you X dollars for our engineer's time." By looking at specific aspects of the deal, it will be easy to slow down the negotiations and keep your counteroffers low. Again, don't forget when you make your concession to ask your customer to give you one in return.

Negotiating successfully is a game of strategy and tactics. Although it takes years of concentrated effort to become a master negotiator, you can certainly increase your effectiveness immediately if you realize one thing: you are valuable to your customers. They want what you are selling, and no matter how much they play the indifferent buyer role, they would not be negotiating with you if they weren't interested in your product or service. Use this knowledge to your advantage and stand your ground. You will be amazed at your results.

CHAPTER ELEVEN

Making the Most at Trade Shows

Tips from a Trade Show Trainer

Julia O'Connor's company, Trade Show Training Inc. (TSTi), is the first company to provide online training to businesses and individuals worldwide that participate in trade-show marketing. She offers several tips for effective trade-show selling.

Understand the difference among the three types of trade shows and where each fits into overall sales and marketing goals and objectives. The most common type of show, general business-to-business, focuses on introductory selling, but not actual selling. Business-to-business shows are where retail and distribution people attend and make purchases. Consumer shows are attended by consumers who buy products and services.

Make sure your trade-show staff are selected and trained in advance. They need expertise on the products exhibited, so they can answer questions and work the demos. They should avoid hard-sales techniques—these scare people away. They should not quote prices on the floor.

Better leads at trade shows start before you get to the show. Define the kind of clients you need. Look at your existing base and the industry demographics to make sure you are on track. Trade shows cut out the equivalent of cold calls because attendees have selected themselves to come to the show and stop by your booth. Knowing all the steps of your firm's sales cycle is critical, so you can place prospects in the appropriate category and not waste time or move them too quickly.

1. *Promote your show in advance with postcards,* ads in trade publications, invitations to the show to hot prospects, and in e-mails. Announce it on your company's Web site. Talk it up to clients and prospects before and after the show.
2. *Upsell clients.* Consider every client a lead for more of your products and services. Never ignore a client at a show—your competitors don't.
3. *Use surveys to learn what your prospects really need.* Design a simple three- to five-item questionnaire with an optional follow-up section. You'll get more honest answers to improve your sales presentations.
4. *Follow up with everyone who stopped by your booth.* An estimated 80 percent of leads are never followed up—a big waste of money for your firm. Even if they are not a good fit now, they will remember the courtesy of a response.
5. *Have a reason to follow up.* When you follow up, answer a question, offer a discount, send a gift—have a reason to continue the dialogue with each present or potential customer.

CHAPTER TWELVE
Keys to Successful Travel

Executive Travel Tips

If you spend a lot of time in airports, you know that flight delays are an inevitable part of the game. The following tips will help you reduce the chances that you'll be stranded.

Always fly nonstop. Every connecting airport you go through is an opportunity for a hold-up.

If you must make connections, allow at least 90 minutes between flights. Otherwise, one delay can set off a domino-chain of missed flights.

Flights early in the morning are the least likely to be delayed. Your next best bet is flights late in the evening. Midmorning to late afternoon is the time of day when you're most apt to run into problems.

Take a carry-on bag with essentials, especially if your trip requires changing planes. Sometimes your baggage doesn't make every connection, even if you do. Even with increased security measures, bad weather is still the most likely reason a flight is delayed or canceled. Check out the "Daily Traveler" link at www.weather.com for updates. If you fly a route frequently, it helps to know where your flight originates, because bad weather in that city could affect your flight.

Check out alternatives in advance. Spend a few minutes online before you go to the airport researching which competing airlines fly to your destination. That way, if you're delayed, you can immediately inquire about available seats on other flights. This information is especially helpful regarding routes you fly on a regular basis.

Never go to the airport without first checking if the flight is on time. Ask again at the check-in desk. If you get to the gate and find your flight has been delayed, you have little choice but to mutter and pace with the other disgruntled passengers. But if you get this information early, you can get the jump on looking for alternatives.

Use Your Travel Time Wisely

Effectively handling time on the road can turn a sales rep from road wearier to road warrior. Following are a few travel tips for using your time on the road wisely and well.

1. **Plan your days early and often** Effective territory management means planning your day of sales calls well in advance. Like a general poring over a map, you should evaluate and plan your territory so that you know which area you'll be visiting days or even weeks ahead of time.
2. **Stay on course** As you look over your day—ideally the night before—roughly estimate how long you want to spend on each call and how long you'll have in between. Of course, you need to be flexible, but as much as possible stick to your schedule.

3. **Rate your customers** How much time you allocate to individual prospects should depend on just how hot they are. Divide your leads into categories of A, B, and C. Then make sure that you're not going out of your way for a C customer or giving too little time to an A customer.
4. **Talk to peers** Territory management may not be a hot topic of collegial conversation, but co-workers and others in the sales field may have terrific tips to help you squeeze the most out of the time you spend on the road.

Essential Readings About Skills

CHAPTER THIRTEEN
Cold Calling for Results

Cold Calls, Hot Selling

How to Make the Most of the Toughest Selling Task

In a perfect world, customers would simply call you up and place large orders. Not only would you have more time to work on your golf game, you'd also avoid the unpleasantness of cold calls. Until that utopia arrives, however, cold calling will remain a necessary evil of the sales profession. In his book *On Selling*, author and International Management Group chairman Mark McCormack offers the following suggestions to light the fire under your cold-calling fingertips.

1. *Excuses, excuses.* Cold calls are always easier when you've got a pretext or excuse for your call. A great reason to call potential customers is if they've just begun a new job. Plus, the new executive is often open to new ideas and options. Look for new job announcements in the local paper or a trade journal, and dial away.

2. *Let's be realistic.* Set modest, achievable goals for your cold-calling efforts. If it's unlikely that you'll make a sale on an individual call, what is a reasonable goal? Maybe it's just getting past the secretary or persuading the customer to let you send some written materials. Downgrade your ambitions and you'll upgrade your spirits when you succeed.
3. *Think top down.* Begin your efforts at the high end of the chain of command. Top executives may be more difficult to reach, but they're also the ones with the influence to buy. Or, they can at least tell you who is the right person to speak with.
4. *Don't lay it on too slick.* When you're making dozens of cold calls, your rap can begin to sound like just that. Alter your routine—even if it's something simple like switching hands on the receiver or standing up—to remind you that each customer is unique and deserves your undivided attention.
5. *Go anywhere for a yes.* Many organizations have people on staff whose job it is to say "No." They tend to have misleading titles like "purchasing agent." Try a different department that's not used to cold calls, like public relations, investor relations, or human resources, and let them help you find your way through the company's organizational chart.

Ten Tips to Effective Cold Calling

Cold calling. Just the name can send chills up your spine. There are effective ways to warm up to cold calling, though, says Barry Nitzberg, director of Enrollment and CRM for Baruch College's Continuing and Professional Studies Division (CAPS) in New York City. He shares 10 tips guaranteed to take the chill off of cold calling.

1. *Define the stages of selling, your selling cycle, and the basics of prospecting.* Understand your selling cycle and the foundations of selling. Know that 90% of your cold call must be spent interviewing your prospect.
2. *Use ratios versus numbers.* Instead of adding more calls to your day, work on improving the ratio of people that you reach. Call executives in the mornings, during lunch or in the evenings. Work on what you say to your prospects to increase the ratio. "Stand up when you're talking," suggests Nitzberg. "Smile when you speak."
3. *Generate leads and turn them into prospects.* "If someone won't speak with you, they are not a prospect," says Nitzberg. "A lead becomes a prospect once they agree to speak with you."
4. *Prepare for effective cold calling.* Have your information organized and your product well defined before you make the initial calls.
5. *Get past the buffers and protectors.* If you call before hours or on Saturdays, you are more likely to get past the gatekeepers and directly to the prospect's voice mail.
6. *Use a great opening script.* First, greet your prospect by name. Second, identify yourself. Third, make a credibility statement regarding your company, products, or services. Fourth, use a reference or allude to a reference. For example, you might say: We work with companies such as Verizon and Sprint. Fifth, state the reason for your call. Here's an example: I'm calling today to make an introductory appointment with you. I'd like to see what your company is doing now and if using some of our services would make sense for you.
7. *Create the necessary level of comfort.* Provide your prospect with the logic and foundation for a conversation. Using a reference helps create comfort.
8. *Make the arrangements.* Ask for the appointment.

9. *Understand and overcome objections and adverse responses.* Be prepared for the usual objections or responses by coming up with responses of your own. Answer an objection with a question. For example, if an individual says, "We aren't interested at this time," you can respond by asking, "Well, what are you doing for ___ right now?"
10. *Follow through.* Schedule your appointment, stick to your schedule, and execute.

Don't Give Up Quickly

There is no hard-and-fast rule as to the number of calls you should make on a prospect before giving up. Many companies keep accurate records on this. They've found that chances for success increase dramatically starting with the fourth or fifth call. The problem is that almost half of all salespeople give up after the first call and only a handful get beyond the second call.

Giving up quickly is hard to understand, given the fact that most customers are happy with their current suppliers and do not switch easily or quickly. A prospect needs compelling reasons to switch, not the least of which is a trusting relationship. Such relationships are seldom established on a single call.

Increasing Chances of Success

Here are eight time-tested tips that will increase chances of success with prospective customers:

1. Follow up immediately on all leads.
2. Qualify the prospect early to determine volume and profit potential.

> 3. Establish your and your company's reputation during the first visit.
> 4. Do more information-gathering than selling on the first call.
> 5. Identify at least two customer needs that your company can fill that are not being satisfied by current supplier(s).
> 6. Don't make the first call a "do or die" situation. Leave the door open for a return visit.
> 7. Always have a good reason to return.
> 8. Schedule a new appointment right away.

Reach for Success

The better your first impression on prospects, the better your chances of getting to make a second one. Just in case your buyers are inclined to make snap judgments as to your character and competence, these tips will help you make a favorable impression.

1. *Keep smiling.* Studies show that we smile only 33 percent of the time that we actually think we're smiling. A cheerful, friendly expression is the greatest predictor of a person's likability. Get in the habit of offering a sincere smile each time you meet your prospects or are introduced to someone new. Your smile might be the one thing that encourages new customers to start up a conversation with you or convinces current ones that you genuinely appreciate their business.
2. *Make eye contact.* Eye contact shows the people you speak with that they have your undivided attention and tells them that you're open and honest with nothing to hide. To project an air of confidence and strength, don't be afraid to look your prospects and customers in the eye. Of course, you can have too much of a good thing—sustained eye contact is

confrontational—so maintain a balance that's inviting and not intimidating.

3. *Make the first move.* Get in the habit of greeting others first instead of waiting for them to greet you. Saying "hello" first marks you as outgoing, confident, and willing to speak even when you aren't spoken to first. Also, prospects might see your willingness to take the initiative as a sign that you won't wait to be asked to do what needs to be done for them and that you care enough about others to extend them a friendly greeting.

4. *Show an interest in others.* Many people are their own favorite topic of conversation. We are all experts on ourselves, and the more we know about a topic, the more comfortable we usually are talking about it. Take an interest in other people, and show your interest by asking questions about them and finding out what you can do to help them. We can all use help from others in our quest for success, and everyone you help may in turn feel obligated to help you.

5. *Offer positive feedback.* You don't have to be a manager or supervisor to let someone know when they're doing a great job. When other members of your sales team close a big sale or finally get an appointment with an important prospect, offer them a verbal pat on the back. The better you make people feel about themselves, the more likely they are to seek out your friendship, which can help you form a valuable network of business contacts and supportive associates.

CHAPTER FOURTEEN
E-mail as a Sales Tool

E-mails That Sell

How to Use E-mail as an Effective Part of Your Sales Process

It may seem simple and obvious. Everyone's under the gun and time is at a premium. E-mail seems like the perfect way to introduce yourself, make your presentation, and at least begin the selling process. But wait... not so fast, say Judith Deal, sales representative at ValPak of Charlotte, North Carolina, and regional sales manager Scott Brien at Netspoke in Woburn, Massachusetts. Both Deal and Brien, who use e-mail extensively, caution sales professionals against using it indiscriminately. If you're considering using e-mail (almost a necessity these days), first understand both its benefits and shortcomings.

Deal finds that the biggest advantage of e-mail is that it allows her to touch people without being intrusive. ValPak is a national company that sells advertising (through coupons that are mailed to households in specified geographic areas) to local businesses in areas served by its ValPak offices. Deal spends her days on the road, talking to potential clients and helping existing customers design their ads. It's easy for busy business owners to resent her interrupting them at work.

"A big advantage of e-mail is that it's not intrusive," she says. "Customers can read your message at their convenience, without being interrupted by you or anyone else. It's a great way to let customers know about special promotions that can allow them to try out our service without a big risk or a firm commitment.

"We have a summer three-month promotion, our 'summer sizzler,' that allows businesses to use us for three months rather than the standard one-year minimum contract. I didn't want to call prospects and intrude on them during a time when they might resent my interrupting them. The solution was e-mail. I just sent a short and gentle e-mail note to potential customers who were not ready for a 12-month commitment, thanking them for their previous interest and offering them the chance to try our service for three months. Businesses are always looking for new customers. I received several calls in response. The customers appreciated my thoughtfulness in keeping them informed of our special offer without bothering them with intrusive calls."

Deal also finds e-mail effective for exchanging ideas with existing and potential customers and sending layouts and proofs to current clients. Her clients can read the information at their leisure and get back to her at their convenience. Sometimes, she sends potential clients a coupon she's designed for a similar business, letting them know how it's been doing and how many responses the existing client has received.

Deal cautions against being too casual when using e-mail. Be professional in your presentation, make sure spelling and grammar are correct, and address the person as Mr. or Ms., not "Jill" or "Bob" (unless, of course the client wants you to address them that way).

Take time to write your e-mail letters carefully. Remember that recipients of an e-mail message will interpret what you say literally, as they cannot see or hear you as they could if you met them in person or called them on the telephone. For that reason, be extra tactful in what you say and how you say it.

Whenever Deal telephones prospects, she always requests their e-mail addresses. "I'm in my car all day, so e-mail saves me a lot of time," she says. When she follows up with information they've requested, news about a special promotion, or a response to a customer's specific needs and concerns, many customers thank her for her thoughtfulness. Deal also uses e-mail to thank customers for their time and provide customer service after a prospect becomes a paying client.

"Find out their needs and what they want, but don't tell them too much," she cautions. "Don't spew your product or service on them."

Brien reinforces Deal's advice about not giving out too much information. Netspoke is a national company, based in Woburn, Massachusetts, that sells Web- and audio-conferencing to small and large businesses. His company receives many requests for information about its services. "I tell our account executives not to assume they know what the customer wants," says Brien. "Instead, they make sure to ask all callers what their specific needs are."

Brien's reps avoid the temptation to give out pricing information too quickly. (Callers often use this information as leverage to launch a bidding war among potential vendors.) They also don't e-mail proposals to prospects. Instead, Brien's reps use Present Express, Netspoke's Web-conferencing service, to application-share a proposal with a prospect. Then the rep and prospect can discuss the proposal while viewing it together.

"One problem account executives face while using e-mail in the sales process," says Brien, "is communicating with a prospect in a manner that has not been completely thought out. It is far too easy for a rep to send prospects a message that doesn't address their specific needs. With e-mail, unlike with a telephone or face-to-face meeting, there can be a lengthy delay between when the initial message is received by the prospect and when the rep can clarify the initial message."

Another danger when using e-mail to advance a sale is that salespeople might make their messages more aggressive than if they were selling over the telephone or in a face-to-face meeting. "This is usually not a successful sales tactic," says Brien. "When using e-mail, there is no immediate way to handle objections, and there is no rapport. Once the prospect has sent their objection, they can easily walk away from their computer and shut down all negotiations.

"Be sure you aren't e-mailing more information than a prospect has requested or needs," cautions Brien. "You need to be as clear and concise as possible: give just enough information to answer the prospect's question, create interest and pique their curiosity, so that they will want to talk to you. That's why we don't send much price or product information in our informational e-mails." To answer general questions, Netspoke has developed templates that are used to generate quick responses, without taking up a rep's time.

Brien's reps craft their e-mails very carefully. Each e-mail message needs to be professional and tactful, give a positive impression about the company, and encourage the rapport-building process between the rep and the prospect. It is important to the company that its sales professionals develop and maintain positive productive relationships with customers. That's why, in e-mail messages, it's important to be even more sensitive and tactful than usual. Brien's reps use e-mail up until the point that it stands in the way of establishing rapport with a prospect.

"Don't use e-mail to replace telephone and face-to-face contact with customers," says Brien. Instead, he recommends using e-mail in the following ways:

"Use e-mail when you have exhausted all chances of telephone or face-to-face contact without getting any response. If a prospect has a genuine need or interest in our product or service, I put 'Netspoke information you requested' in the subject line of my e-mail message. Be sure to get a receipt, so you know that the addressee has actually opened your message."

Brien cautions sales professionals not to use e-mail excessively early on in the sales process. Instead, he recommends using it to keep in touch with prospects once rapport has been established. Then e-mail can be a convenient and time-saving way to share information, exchange ideas, and provide personalized customer service after the sale.

How to Use E-mail to Build and Maintain Relationships

Jack Burke, president of Sound Marketing Inc. and author of *Relationship Aspect Marketing* and *Creating Customer Connections*, says e-mail's major advantages are speed of delivery and efficiency. Disadvantages result from a tendency toward spam and lack of common courtesy. Because e-mail is free, many people abuse it by sending forwarded jokes, "good thoughts," chain e-mail, and editorial observations.

Burke's Air Force colonel brother-in-law marvels over the electronic accessibility to senior officers formerly guarded by secretarial staffs. He also is amazed at how many generals cannot write or spell correctly. Remember every communication reflects back on the person sending it.

On the positive side, Burke applauds ProgramBusiness.com. This Internet site, serving insurance agents and brokers, registers more than a million hits a month and has a strong advertiser base without ever having spent a penny in traditional advertising. Its success has been the result of a free electronic newsletter e-mailed to the insurance community every two weeks. The e-mail database includes

30,000 agents and brokers that have elected to receive the newsletter due to the value of the information provided. Everything is based on permission marketing.

Here are Burke's guidelines for improving your e-mail techniques to maintain existing relationships and prospect for new ones:

1. *Always provide value first.* Blatant sales pitches may harvest some low-hanging fruit, but effective selling should be based on value that earns you the right to their business.
2. *Seek permission to provide ongoing information.*
3. *Provide contact information* so recipients can reply in the medium of their choice.
4. *Keep the e-mail basic*—avoid attachments and HTML graphics that take time to load. Some people are still on the slower dial-up modem connections.
5. *Use hyperlinks* to allow recipients to access more complete information, which can be mounted on your Web site.
6. *Be courteous!* Use salutatory openings and closings, watch your grammar, and check your spelling.
7. *Resist the temptation* to forward jokes and other nonpertinent messages.
8. *Continually build* your database of e-mail addresses.
9. *Provide a subject line* that truly informs the recipient of what the message contains.

CHAPTER FIFTEEN

Getting Attention with Sales Letters

Energize Your Sales Letters

"The sales letter," says Nader Anise, International Lecturer and MBA professor at Nova Southeastern University, "is a tried-and-true way to make an offer. To be effective, it should capture interest within five seconds and direct the prospect to a desired action."

Professor Anise cites five ways to accomplish this purpose.

1. *Begin your letter with a sharp one-liner.* Whether a statement or question, this should be as intriguing and benefit-oriented as possible. For example: "Here's a way to increase your company's bottom line by 30 percent"; or, "Do you want to shine with your boss?"
2. *Adopt a reader-friendly tone.* Too many reps make sales letters sound like doctoral dissertations. The best letters are relaxed and informal, as if you're writing to a friend or close relative. Avoid polysyllabic words. Make your letters sound conversational.

3. *Give your letter visual appeal.* The easier and faster to read, the better. Avoid long, drawn-out sentences. Use bullets or numbers when making a list. Italicize important points and words or set them in bold type. Limit paragraph length to six lines. Use short simple sentences.
4. *Stress benefits.* Don't make the customer ask, "Why am I reading this?" Keep repeating his or her payoff. Make your letters you-centered as opposed to me-centered.
5. *Tell prospects what you want them to do at least four times.* The sales letter should be designed to trigger action. Do you want the customer to call your toll-free number or reply by e-mail? Work the number or e-mail address into the letter again and again. Repetition with desired action in mind is not only acceptable, it's also essential.

It's All in How You Say It

It's been well established by behavioral science that what we say—and how we say it—has a tremendous impact on thoughts and actions. Yet according to author Dr. Kenneth Christian, many of us go about our lives woefully unaware of the impact everyday use of language has on our attitudes and our fundamental beliefs about ourselves. In *Your Own Worst Enemy: Breaking the Habit of Adult Underachievement*, Christian offers six tips for taking control of your speech patterns and talking yourself into greater achievement.

1. *Stop "try"-ing.* The word *try* is a part of what Christian calls "loophole language." By saying you will *try* to do something, you are implicitly giving yourself an out to fall short. For one week, forbid yourself to use the word *try* and see what kind of

effect it has. Also, note the difference you feel between forbidding yourself to use the word and simply "trying" not to.

2. *Cut out vagueness.* Phrases like *kind of* and *sort of* allow you to express ambivalence while seeming to make a statement. When you speak about goals or other definitive aspects of your life, use unequivocal language. Don't say, "I sort of want to do this," say, "I will do this."

3. *Take responsibility.* Decisive people, you'll notice, speak simply, in the present tense and in the active voice. Compare the difference between "It needs to get done" and "I need to do it." Take greater personal responsibility with your language, and you will take greater personal responsibility with your life.

4. *Negate the negative.* Catch yourself every time you use such self-defeating statements as "I hate making presentations," "It's too late to take this training," or "I can't figure out this new computer system." Such self-limiting talk becomes a self-fulfilling prophesy. Instead, say, "I choose to like making presentations," "There's still time to take the training," and "I have yet to figure out the new training." Ask your friends and family to help catch you whenever you use negative phrases.

5. *Put things behind you.* Describe any negative traits you perceive about yourself in the past tense. So rather than saying "I'm not a good closer," say "I didn't used to be a good closer." By relegating these negative attributes to the past, you imply the possibility for change, and soon you'll be believing it.

6. *Make positives present.* Use the present tense to discuss positive attributes, even one you don't feel you manifest quite yet. By using the present tense, you put pressure on yourself to make the statement a reality.

CHAPTER SIXTEEN
Leaving Effective Voice Mails

Prospecting and Voice-Mail Tips That Work

Even in the Internet age, some of the best prospecting tactics remain decidedly low-tech. So says Linda Dabrea, sales manager with Unifirst Corporation, a work garment company in western Massachusetts. While she admits her sales team uses the Web to troll for new business, she also recognizes the value of keeping one's selling ear to the ground.

"We service, rent, and lease work garments," Dabrea says. "Part of our business is uniforms traditionally associated with heavy-soil environments (heavy machinery, auto body repair, etc.), but part is also garments designed to promote a specific corporate image in the service sector. That might mean something as simple as Dockers-style pants and an oxford shirt with the corporate logo or a name embroidered on it.

"The newspaper is a good source for possible new business. If a local company is hiring and in its ad offers as a benefit an employee work garment program, that company is a prime candidate for our services. And the papers frequently run articles profiling local businesses, which can also give us a heads up. Besides that, if we see a company with a lot of delivery trucks on the roads, then we know that company has employees going into customers' places of business and may be interested in creating a recognizable team work garment—sort of like you see with UPS. When it comes to prospecting, just paying attention to what's going on around you can pay dividends."

Identifying target accounts is one challenge; another is getting in to meet the prospect. Rather than leaving an endless series of unreturned machine messages, Dabrea recommends tapping into the current quiz show craze to coax that coveted return call.

"We try not to leave the standard 'This is so-and-so from such-and-such company' message because you never get a return call that way, and you wind up frustrated," she explains. "Instead, I suggest our reps phrase the messages in the same way our customers frequently ask us questions about the industry. So I might say, 'Hi, this is Linda from Unifirst. I thought you might like to know the answer to the following question: What is the best single motivator for your employees coming to work in a heavy-soil environment? If you'd like to know the answer please call me back at this number.'

"It's a way to differentiate yourself from the parade of voice mails that every customer gets. It may be just the thing to make someone say, 'That sounds interesting. Let me call them back and see what that's all about.'"

What Voice Messages Actually Get Customers to Call You Back?

"When you're catching someone live or on voice mail, you have a window of opportunity of only 20 to 30 seconds to distinguish yourself," says Marc Baum, national business development manager for the Canterbury Consulting Group (www.canterburycorpuniv.com), a comprehensive blended-solutions training provider offering Softskill, Business Systems/Enterprise, and Technical/Application training.

"Whether they'll talk longer with me, let me send them information, or arrange for a face-to-face, this dialogue needs to leave me standing apart from my competitors."

For him, a script is essential. "I don't mean a canned script," explains Baum. "It has to be delivered in conversational language, and it has to entice the receiver to hear more. I have to come across as credible; I have to understand this individual's pain. And I have to lead them into the wiifem (what's in it for them)."

The key is to focus on solving a problem for them, rather than selling a product or service. This will improve your chances of getting them to call back. If you already have them on the phone, it's more likely that that they will listen to what you have to say because they know that you have a handle on their situation.

Of course, Baum concedes, sometimes there is greater urgency to reach an individual. When that's the case, he recommends calling early or late—at 7:30 in the morning or maybe 7:30 at night. "Key people," he says, "work long hours."

As an agent account executive for U.S. Cellular, Diana Uphold knows her way around the telephone dial. She sends off a group voice-mail to her agent/owners and all their employees every morning and gets roughly an 85 percent response. "It didn't happen overnight," says Uphold. "This has been a year-long process. We got a new manager who helped us refocus our energy and get more buy-in from the agents. I think we get so many call-backs because we have focused on really keeping in touch and making them understand how important it is."

Of course, since Uphold's in the business of selling voice mail, her group voice mails have an added significance. "If you don't use it, you don't sell it," she says. "Sometimes the basis of a call is just to motivate the employees to sell our products. We get reports every single day on what every location did—how many cell phones, how many voice mails and other vertical were sold the day before."

Because she uses voice mail so much, with the same customers over and over again, Uphold has to be especially careful about crafting her messages so that each one seems distinct. Sometimes she'll leave a motivational quote. Other times she uses voice messaging to update agents on emergencies like a tower going down and cutting off service. But most of the time, she's just trying to get her agents to think about voice mail and selling more verticals. "We try to personalize group voice mails with an individual message like, 'That was a great job you did yesterday,'" she says. "Many times we'll talk about a special feature we've been promoting all month, but with a different angle."

Key Voice Mail Skills

1. Practice makes perfect and cuts down on the "umms" and "uhhs" that make people reach for the delete button before you even finish.
2. Be sure to leave your phone number and remember to say it slowly and clearly. It makes it easier for the client to call you back.
3. Prospects are looking for solutions, not products. So focus your message on an idea you have that can help.
4. Personalize your message so that it doesn't sound like a scripted or group call.
5. Build in an air of mystery, so the client will be curious about calling you back.

CHAPTER SEVENTEEN
Keys for Strong Communications

Mirror, Mirror, on the Call

Use Reflective Techniques to Become a More Effective Communicator

Feedback helped some of the great psychadelic rock bands of the 1960s create a unique sound that helped shape a generation. Feedback, when used effectively, can also help sales professionals deal with their customers, colleagues, and managers. In *Artful Persuasion*, author Harry Mills suggests the following tips for mastering the art of giving reflective feedback.

1. *Reflective listening.* Of course, the most critical initial step in delivering feedback is to listen. While you listen, consider both the message the person is conveying as well as the feelings behind message.

2. *Reflecting content.* What is the essence of what the other person is saying to you? Can you boil it down to one or two sentences that cut through the clutter and then reflect back what the person is trying to communicate? Remember, don't simply repeat verbatim what you've just heard—that will simply stunt the conversation. Use opening phrases like:

- It sounds like ...
- In other words ...
- So ...
- So, you're saying ...
- It seems that ...
- Do you mean ...
- I guess ...

3. *Reflecting feelings.* People who speak in emotional tones want their feelings acknowledged. For example, when a customer complains about how much more paperwork she has to deal with today compared with five years ago, you might respond by saying, "It sounds like you're frustrated with the increased level of bureaucracy."

By practicing reflective listening and delivering effective feedback, you will

- Encourage others to continue talking
- Resolve misunderstandings, false assumptions, and misinterpretations
- Reassure others that you are paying attention
- Gain a more in-depth understanding of other people's needs
- Remember more of what people say to you
- Build rapport and gain the respect of those you work with

Seven Tips on Giving and Receiving a Compliment

Giving or receiving a compliment or saying "thank you" to a prospect can be tricky business. How do you do it without sounding insincere or condescending? Humphries offers these guidelines for the fine art of saying "thank you."

1. *Give compliments one at a time.* Otherwise, you'll sound gushy.
2. *Keep your compliment to the scale of the event.* Don't gush on and on if the situation doesn't warrant it. Otherwise, you'll sound like you're complimenting them to "butter 'em up."
3. *Compliment for a reason.* Make sure your compliment is for some action your prospect has taken and not given to make yourself look good. Otherwise, your prospect will see through the compliment and it will backfire.
4. *Learn the art of accepting a compliment graciously.* Pause, say "Thank you," and nothing else.
5. *Say "Thank you" for a reasonable compliment.* Otherwise, deflect it by changing the subject. Insincere flattery should put you on the alert.
6. *If your client pays you a compliment and it is well deserved, consider this response.* Say casually, "Thanks, but that's the way we do business." This response reinforces the positive sales experience your client has enjoyed.
7. *Don't compliment prospects on how they look.* It's too personal a comment and not appropriate in a business setting. Women especially are tired of being recognized only for appearance. Instead, say something complimentary about the prospect's product, office, or staff. One caution: Be sincere.

CHAPTER EIGHTEEN
Follow-up Strategies

Do You Clean Up or Give Up on Follow-up?

The best salesperson I ever knew seldom did much prospecting. If that sounds like the ultimate heresy, so be it, because this salesman was nearly three times more productive than the national average of his peers. What he did in place of the traditional prospecting routines was to conduct a very careful follow-up of his customers.

And they did his prospecting for him!

Many salespeople fail to consider why they walked into a certain account and took business away from a competitor. Was it because their product was superior? Perhaps, but most products are fairly competitively matched in quality, function, and price, and buyers can generally move from one to another with considerable ease. Was it because they gave such a splendid presentation? Maybe. Certainly it had to be good enough to turn the buyer from a neutral to a positive position, but then buyers are exposed to good presentations all the time.

How about trying this scenario: You walk into ABC & Co. with the objective of unseating your competitor. You have never even gotten to first base with these people; they are polite but keep telling you that their needs are well cared for... come back another time. So you do, and this time you present a secondary-type or specialty item—just a minor product your competitor pays little attention to. And, what do you know... you make the sale!

The following day, you send a card to the buyer, confirming the shipping date you had promised and thanking him for the order. A week later, the order is shipped. You give the buyer a call and tell him that the order is on its way. A few days later, you call and ask if the order has been received and whether the product is working properly.

Two weeks later, you're in the customer's area once again, and you drop in to see him. "I just wanted to make sure that everything is okay," you say. And the customer says, "It's working just fine. You people carry a line of... (he mentions your bread-and-butter product) don't you?"

You tell him that you certainly do and ask if they would like to order some. The customer says, "Send me a trial order... we'd like to give it a closer look."

So you do. And you go through the exact routine you did before, except this time you run into a snag!

The problem is that ABC & Co. has always used your competitor's product, which has certain characteristics that differ from yours. In using the sample shipment, the operators failed to read the instructions clearly printed on the package. The results: bad. Because your product is compounded in such a way that less of it is needed than that of your competitor's (a point you have always made in your sales presentations), their trial run was a disaster. Now what do you do?

"Sweet are the uses of adversity," someone once said. Problems solved are triumphs; unsolved, they are disasters. If we sell well, we should be looking for problems to solve—even if they are problems our own product helped create.

Back to your victory-turned-sour. The complaint has been discovered early enough for your remedial action to be effective. You now have an opportunity to get out into the shop and to talk to the people who are having the problem. You show them the differences in your product and that of your competitor, and you hang on until they have completed another trial run. The results are superb!

ABC & Co. continues to use your competitor's product, but you get a few small reorders. You check back to see how it's going. And then the orders get larger. Months later, you're having lunch with the buyer at ABC & Co. and he lets you in on the reason for the switch: You followed up, and your competitor didn't.

Obviously, as your customer list grows, your follow-up efforts increase. The easy way to keep abreast of your own success is to organize yourself to do it. Here are a few suggestions:

- On a new sale, send a follow-up note of appreciation the following day. Then mark your calendar for the important dates to come—delivery date, check-up date, reorder date.
- In addition to these calendar notes, make a few others. If the account isn't regularly active, how about a quarterly follow-up?
- Do you know your buyer's birthdate? How about a birthday card—an easy annual contact to make.
- Develop a list of customers and the products they buy. Break this into product lists, and when any change in product application or price comes up, the notices can be sent automatically.
- Route-schedule so that you can call on inactive accounts on your way to active accounts.

Time has always been an important factor to salespeople. It has become a major cost factor to management in recent years; the cost of a sales call has gone soaring. To save both time and money, the modern salesperson has to develop good telephone and note-writing techniques. To be sure, there are poor substitutes for the personal contact, but, in many instances, they are better than widely spaced contacts.

Here's a handy checklist for follow-up calls:

1. *Plan follow-up.* That means scheduling and it also means deciding in advance what is to be said.
2. *Always have a good reason for calling.* You want to find out if the product is working properly; there's a new application that the customer should know about; a new price has been announced, and so forth.
3. *Make follow-up calls short.* Your customer has a lot more to do than talk to you.
4. *If you are making a call in person, make an appointment.* Drop-ins are sometimes welcome, sometimes not. Knowing your customer's schedule and habits will give you guidance in this.
5. *If a problem arises, handle it.* If you make a phone call, and there's a problem that can't be cared for on the spot, make an appointment and pack a bag.

Follow-up, of course, doesn't preclude the necessity for prospecting, but it certainly makes it a lot easier. And the nice thing about following up is that when you do prospect for new business, you're adding to your customer list, not replacing someone on it.

Your best selling opportunities, indeed, come after the sale.

The simple truth is that it is easier to convince a salesperson to make a follow-up call in pursuit of new business than it is to convince him or her to follow-up with regular customers.

This doesn't make sense, and here's why:

- It's easier to maintain a relationship than to begin one.
- What was worth going after in the first place is worth preserving.

- If you don't pay attention to your customer, he or she will find someone else who will.
- Referrals from satisfied customers turn cold calls into hot prospects.

That last item is often the most difficult to believe, but it happens. Salespeople—if they're either very good or very bad—get talked about. At meetings of business associations, chambers of commerce, at social gatherings, at the first tee on the golf course, in local bars and restaurants, the "Do-you-know-Charlie?" routine goes on and on. It's the follow-up salesperson who gets talked about most...most favorably.

They are the real estate salespeople who call to find out if the family is comfortable in the new home...car salesmen who call to find out if the new car is performing properly...industrial salespeople who call to find out if the shipment arrived in good shape and on time. My wife recently had a short stay at a local hospital, and three days after she got home the hospital administrator called to find out how she was feeling. The doctor never bothered. But you can imagine how well talked-up that hospital is these days!

Pasted inside every salesperson's hat should be these words:

NEVER FORGET A CUSTOMER...AND NEVER LET A CUSTOMER FORGET YOU!

CHAPTER NINETEEN
Writing Winning Proposals

Writing Better Proposals

Many salespeople consider writing either (a) a boring class they took in college, (b) a time waster, better left to a secretary, or (c) unimportant and best gotten out of the way as quickly as possible.

Few salespeople realize the persuasive power of a strong written proposal. Many salespeople cling to the idea that effective writing skills are unnecessary. "Look," they reason, "I'm paid to talk and sell. That has nothing to do with writing."

Yes, but think how much more you could sell if you could talk and write. Then you could sell to prospects over the phone, in person, and through writing.

Below are four ways to make your sales-writing skills as strong as your verbal selling skills. These are essential keys to strong proposal writing.

1. *Small, familiar words.* Your first goal as writer is to be clear to the reader. The best way to do that is by using small, familiar

words. As a rule of thumb, if you have to choose between a large word and a small word, pick the small word every time.

For example, don't use *endeavor* when you can say *try*. Don't use *terminate* when you can say *end* or *commence* when you can say *begin*.

Small words are not only more understandable and exact than large words, they also add elegance to your writing.

When Neil Armstrong set foot on the moon, he didn't give a speech about the meaning of that awesome moment. He simply said: "That's one small step for a man, one giant leap for mankind." A poet could not have spoken with more eloquence.

2. *Short, simple sentences.* Keep your sentences short and simple. Like small, familiar words, they're easier to read and understand. They're also easier to write. Generally, a sentence should average about 15 to 20 words. But don't assume that all sentences must fall within that range. It's best to vary sentence length. Intersperse sentences of 25 words with shorter ones.

Just as you mustn't overload a sentence with unnecessary words, you also shouldn't pack a sentence with too many ideas. A sentence should contain one or two ideas at most. That way, the reader won't lose your meaning.

3. *Active-voice verbs.* Use active-voice verbs whenever possible. They give your writing more clarity and emphasis. What is the active voice?

When a verb is in the active voice, the subject of the sentence performs the action. For example, "The batter hit the ball." But when it's passive, the subject receives the action of the verb: "The ball was hit by the batter."

Take for example the sales manager's memo that said: "Expense accounts must be submitted by month's end."

Here's the problem. By using the passive voice, the sales manager did not identify who should submit their expense accounts, so he didn't receive any. But he received all of them when he rewrote the memo in the active voice: "New salespeople must submit expense accounts by month's end."

4. *Conversational style.* Strive for a natural, conversational style. On one hand don't use slang, but on the other hand avoid stiff formality. Not long ago, a salesperson sent a form letter to customers that read: "There has been an affirmative decision for program termination."

Many customers called the home office asking what the letter meant. The company could have avoided the problem if it had said in the letter: "The company decided to end the program."

Don't shy away from using *I'll* and *you'll* in your business writing. For example, don't start a business letter with: "Enclosed herewith is the requested information." The writer could have made a better impression with: "I have attached the information you requested."

Use these four tips in your business writing, and I'm confident your memos, letters, reports, and proposals will attract the attention and produce the results they deserve.

Packing Persuasion in Your Writing

"To be successful at persuasion, what we write or say should influence what the audience thinks, how they feel or what they do," says Tom Sant in the second edition of *Persuasive Business Proposals: Writing to Win More Customers, Clients, and Contracts.*

In his book, Sant gives a practical approach to writing persuasively. He calls this effective four-step pattern for persuasion the Persuasive Paradigm.

1. *State customers' needs.* It's very important to demonstrate that you understand your customers' needs. If you don't do this up front, customers have no reason to listen to what you have to say. Summarize the business situation briefly, focusing on the gap to be closed or the competency to be acquired. "By showing customers that you get it, that you listened to them and understood what they told you, you raise their level of confidence," says Sant.
2. *Identify the positive outcomes.* How do your customers measure success? What makes your product worth it? Your goal is motivation. "If we don't create a sense of urgency in the decision maker to go forward with our recommendation, we have not been successful in our persuasion effort," says Sant. "You create a sense of motivation in your customers by showing that the problem you are addressing is really one that should be fixed. Focus on customers' pain to get their attention; focus on their gain to get their commitment."
3. *Recommend a solution.* Link the product or service to customers' specific problems. Believe in your solution; don't be wishy-washy, says Sant. He recommends using words such as: "We urge you . . .." or "We are confident . . . ."
4. *Prove that you can do it.* Any company can say it can solve a problem. It's up to you to prove it to your customers. How? Provide details to substantiate your claim. Use references, testimonials, case studies, guarantees, and details about your management philosophy and company history.

CHAPTER TWENTY
Handling Objections

Proven Strategies for Getting Over the Rejection Hump

You can tell the difference between successful and unsuccessful sales professionals by the way they handle rejection. Top performers seem almost immune to the stuff, whereas their underachieving counterparts can't help but absorb the painful slings and arrows of unsympathetic customers. As a real estate agent since the Reagan administration and a manager with O'Brien Realty in Solomons, Maryland, Judy Szynborski has faced more rejection than a jockey playing one-on-one basketball with Shaquille O'Neal. The following are Szynborski's four key tips for dealing with rejection.

1. *Back it up.* "Sometimes customers don't want to disclose information to you, so they react with a rejection because they're in denial or they're uncomfortable answering some of the questions you've asked. If they don't know what's happening, inexperienced agents tend to feel rejected. But an experienced agent will pick up on the body language and signals much more quickly. They'll back up, reroute the line of questioning and go

at the customer from a completely different angle. This is a good way experienced reps reduce the rejection they face."

2. *Get pumped.* "Listening to motivational tapes is a great help. Find a particular tape that you're comfortable with, then keep it in your car. Then, when you've had a day filled with rejection, pop the tape in and just listen. All of a sudden it gives you perspective, and empowers you to step back into the ring knowing it's not about you."

3. *Innocently inquire.* "When a customer rejects you and the sale is lost, try to put a human face on it. Ask the customer, 'Is it something I did?' Most people will say, 'No, it wasn't you' and then tell you what the real issue is. And then you can get to what the real objection is and possibly salvage the sale."

4. *Take a number.* "Top performers know that there are some situations they just can't do anything about—that you just have to move on. Learn to say, 'Next!' like you're working behind the deli counter. You just say, 'I don't know what's going on here, but I don't have time to figure it out. Next!' After facing a series of rejections you tend to put your guard up, but then someone really nice comes along and makes up for it. But you have to pick up the phone and give that person the opportunity to do that for you."

Price Squad

Tips for Combating the Ubiquitous Price Objection

On a frustration scale of 1 to 10, most salespeople would rate the price objection at about an 11. No question, buyers love to beat us up on price. Luckily, there are many effective methods for dealing with the sticky price issue, many of which do not involve taking hostages.

Mark Pawelski, a sales manager with Riverside Color Corporation, a Minneapolis digital prepress facility, suggests the following tips that he says have worked for his sales team:

1. *First call, an information call.* "I like to get all the information we can on the first call by asking, 'How are your files built, why do you use a certain software and so on.' We don't try to sell them anything, so price doesn't come up. We can take all that information we've gathered back and discuss the right approach, then get back to the customer to say, 'Here's where we're at.'"
2. *Don't give them a price list.* "Every job we do is a custom job, so we don't have a set price list. Our price depends on a variety of factors—how ready is the customer's work, what's the volume, what type of job it is—so we don't like to give a price list up front. If the customer asks, we say, 'We don't have a price list that we pass out. We want to be involved in every aspect of quoting this job. We need to look at what you have, figure out what's unique about the job, and bring to your attention some things that can save you money, which you wouldn't be able to do based on a price list.' Sometimes it works, sometimes it doesn't. But we always begin by trying to get the customer to understand everything that goes into our pricing."
3. *You want it cheap? No kidding*! "As soon as someone says, 'We need it fast and we need it cheap,' we always say, 'Great, everybody is in the same boat; that's why we're set up the way we are—to save you money and time.' We address their quick turnaround issues by discussing our staffing and processes. We also bring up volume. We can do a lot better on price if we do 50 of something instead of one. So we use their price needs to press for quantity."

4. *Okay, give them a price list.* "If a customer insists, and it's a high-volume job, sometimes we will give them a price list, with the prices cut substantially, because it's the only way to get them in the door. Even though we don't know how the work will go, or what the job consists of, at least this way we can establish the relationship. Then we can figure out whether we can find a way to adjust our work flow to hit our profit margin at the prices we're charging. And if we can't make any money, we can always walk away."
5. *Stick with it.* "The first thing buyers learn in buying school is to ask for everything fast and cheap, hoping that this will weed out half the people right away. Often, if you can just get past that point to begin identifying why they wanted to see you and what they're not getting from the current supplier, you can meet their needs, whatever they are, and find out what their so-called 'pain' is. When you get to that level of understanding, price becomes much less of an issue."

Price Versus Value

Experts always say, "Focus on value, not on price." However, customers don't always listen to the experts. So if your customers want to talk price, simply put a price tag on the value you offer. Go over the following with price-conscious buyers:

1. What are the benefits you offer that are most valuable to your customers—time saved, reduced labor costs, speedier delivery?
2. Calculate how much each of these benefits will save your customers on a monthly, quarterly, or annual basis.

> 3. By sacrificing these benefits, what costs will the customers accrue?
> 4. Compare the one-time price of your product or service with the long-term savings.

Chase Down the Evaders

Tips for Selling to the Most Elusive of Customers

Difficult customers are a fact of life in sales. To get signed contracts from them, you must develop strategies to work beyond the difficulties—either that or risk running afoul of our nation's strict forgery statutes. In the *K.I.S.S. Guide To Selling,* authors Ken Lloyd and Gloria Anderson identify "Evaders" as one of the most challenging customer categories facing most sales reps. The authors break down the category into six specific types and offer the following suggestions for dealing with each:

Evader No. 1: The Duck

Characteristics: Avoids your calls and never responds to phone messages.
Strategy: Go duck hunting. Call during off-business hours, like early in the morning, after 6 p.m., or on weekends. Try a variety of media contacts. Besides voice mail, how about an e-mail newsletter? Can you send something via snail mail that will be of interest to the prospect, like a recent magazine article or letter of reference?

Evader No. 2: The Torpedo

Characteristics: Cancels meetings at the last minute.
Strategy: Try to set appointments for Tuesday, Wednesday, or Thursday, preferably in the morning. Prospects are typically dealing with a weekend's worth of work on Mondays, and Fridays tend to be low energy. Also, as torpedoes often cancel appointments because they don't understand the benefits you offer, try to keep the potential value you offer in their minds between the day you set the appointment and the day you arrive to present.

Evader No. 3: The Short Cutter

Characteristics: Abruptly ends meetings with you.
Strategy: Present the key values you offer early in the meeting. If the prospect cuts you short, don't get discouraged. Most sales take more than one call anyway. Use your flexibility to show the customer you're willing to adapt, but get a commitment for another meeting in the near future.

Evader No. 4: The Delay of Gamer

Characteristics: Keeps you waiting beyond the scheduled meeting time.
Strategy: Don't get upset or angry. Plan your schedule with enough flexibility that you can use the extra time for paperwork, returning phone calls or preparing yourself some more for the call itself.

Evader No. 5: The Slow Speaker

Characteristics: Speaks . . . very . . . slowly . . . and . . . deliberate . . . ly
Strategy: Adjust your speech to match the customer's pace. Even if it's excruciating for you, and you fear that your heart will stop

beating altogether, force yourself to slow down. The customer will be reassured and put at ease by the slower tempo.

Evader No. 6: The Wall

Characteristics: Quiet and seemingly uninterested in what you're saying.
Strategy: Ask open-ended questions and then wait for the reply. If this means enduring long periods of silence, so be it. Wait them out and these prospects will typically offer very thoughtful, thorough answers to your questions.

CHAPTER TWENTY-ONE
Closing Essentials

As Time Goes—Buy

Advice for Motivating Your Reluctant Customers to Buy

According to Josh Gordon, author of *Tough Calls*, nearly half of all sales professionals report difficulty dealing with indecisive customers. The following are some of Gordon's proven tips to inspire your fence-straddling prospects to overcome their fears and make a decision.

1. *Time is money.* For putting a little life into your customers, nothing beats a deadline. Provide an incentive (discount, upgrade, free sample, etc.) if customers act by a certain date, and they frequently will find the initiative. Also, your prospects can use the deadline to persuade others within the buying organization that the time is ripe to act.
2. *Take me for granted—please!* Try to create a buying pattern where clients make purchases at the same time every month, season, or year. If you can convince buyers to act consistently, you can make that decision a given. Indecisive customers will

feel as though they aren't really making the decision, thus paving the way for your sale.
3. *Up the ante.* Small orders are small decisions. Paradoxically, many reluctant customers feel more comfortable making larger decisions as members of a buying group than on their own. Balloon the size of your order and you may actually take the burden off your contacts by requiring that more people participate in the decision.
4. *Be the security blanket.* Indecisive customers are frequently insecure. One way to address their concerns is with information. Provide a barrage of industry data, customer testimonials, and any other persuasive material you can muster. Then let the customers know you are willing to take responsibility for the success of the project and that your credibility is on the line. Your confidence will rub off and make the buying decision easier.
5. *Get to "No."* Sometimes customers don't want to say no, so they stall and act indecisively when they know they aren't going to buy. Ask directly if this is the case. If customers are honest and say yes, you know you can stop wasting your time. Or, if the customers are surprised and a bit taken aback, this tactic can be just what you need to push them into a buying mode.

Ready to Close

Is your prospect ready to sign on the dotted line? Sales consultants often counsel salespeople to close early and often. But what's the hurry? Maybe waiting for your prospect to show some closing signs isn't a bad idea. The quiz below can help guide you in your quest for the close.

Answer YES or NO

1. Are you convinced of the prospect's genuine need for the product or service?
2. Did the prospect make the initial contact?
3. Did the prospect agree to the interview after seeing your literature?
4. Is the prospect pumping you for information not germane to the interview?
5. Are you the first salesperson the prospect has seen?
6. Did the prospect wince when you mentioned price?
7. Have you established good rapport with the prospect?
8. Has the prospect discussed delivery options?
9. Can you think of any objections that you have not resolved?
10. Has the prospect talked about a buying schedule?

Is the prospect ready to sign? What do your YES or NO answers signify?

1. YES: If convinced of the buyer's need, you're ahead of the game.
2. YES: It's a good sign if the buyer contacted you.
3. YES: Highly favorable. If the prospect wasn't impressed by your literature, you wouldn't have had the interview.
4. YES: Could mean problems. Prospects have been known to see salespeople simply to pump them for information.
5. YES: It's hard to close fast if you're the first sales rep interviewed; your work may still be cut out for you.
6. YES: Don't be discouraged; price wince could be no more than a reflex response.
7. YES: With good rapport, you're always well ahead of the game.

> 8. YES: Interest expressed in delivery usually means prospects are ready to close whether they know it or not.
> 9. YES: Always a big bugaboo. If you suspect an objection remains, discuss it before reaching for your pen.
> 10. YES: This is a definite buying signal. Go for it.

Upsell to a Win–Win Conclusion

"First of all, I think it's a proven maxim that most salespeople undersell, not oversell, especially when they're in the rookie venue," says sales consultant Robbie Brown, president of R.L. Brown & Associates, a consulting firm specializing in profit maximization. "They justify the behavior by saying, 'I got the sale and that's the most important thing.'"

Brown feels one of the reasons salespeople don't upsell is that they don't take the time to qualify and understand the real needs of the customer.

"It brings us back to Selling 101," Brown explains. "Regardless of what you're selling, you need to go through the basic qualification process—not only the actual needs, but the customer passion and sophistication that goes along with them. For example, let's say you sell sport utility vehicles. If the buyer is a suburban mom and a first-time buyer, she'll have one set of needs. If the buyer is a passionate camper who goes to the mountains every weekend, that person will have a different set of needs. Obviously, with a first-time buyer you don't want to be guilty of overkill. On the other hand, if you don't offer options and try to move the customer up the ladder, you're guilty of underselling."

Brown adds, "Have an in-depth conversation to determine what the customer should buy, and be smart enough to listen. A common fault of salespeople is rushing to tell the customer all they know, instead of the other way around."

Brown thinks another mistake salespeople make is not starting at the right price point.

"Where some salespeople go afoul is with 'step up' selling—starting at the entry-level price and then trying to move the customer up to a higher price versus starting at the top and moving down.

"A buyer will typically move only two price points. If you're selling a product with five different pricing options, and you begin the process at the entry level, you may move two price points up. If you start at the top you may move down one or two points, but you're still going to be on a higher level.

"Keep in mind the sophistication of the buyers, and don't presume to know what they want," says Brown. "For example, if I own two and one-half acres of lawn, I'm probably not interested in looking at a basic push mower. And most people don't want to buy junk. They want the best value they can get for the money they can spend, and it's up to the salesperson to move them to the appropriate product level."

Brown believes part of the reason more salespeople don't upsell, in addition to their failing to recognize the customer's need for ancillary products, is that management doesn't provide suitable sales training. "Part of the problem lies in organizations where sales training is really product training," Brown points out. "Learning all the features and benefits of a product is important, but it's not the same as learning how to sell the product. They are two different subjects altogether.

"Salespeople need to remember they don't sell products, they sell results. People don't really want to buy solvents—they want to buy clean floors and everything that goes along with them. What could be worse than the customer buying a product, all excited, only to find out it doesn't perform as expected because a certain accessory was needed and the salesperson never offered it. That customer is not going to be a happy camper, because the salesperson sold only what was asked for, not what was really needed. In almost any sales scenario, there are ancillary products that can be offered, even if the customer didn't ask to see them.

"When the buyer walks away with a thinner wallet, but with a smile, your customer's won and you've won," says Brown.

CHAPTER TWENTY-TWO
Teleselling Skills

Telephone Selling

Perseverance, Prioritizing, and Planning Can Do Away with Phone Tag

You want to contact a prospect to finalize a sale or you want to let good customers know about a special deal that can save them money. But there's a problem—you can never reach the person by telephone. At the same time, your customer gets only your voice mail or an assistant when returning your call. What can you do?

"Make it possible for your customers to reach a live person—even when you aren't available," advises Eric Harris, sales manager at Benefit Partners in Roseville, California, a third-party administrator that offers independent insurance agents ("brokers") and their customers access to a wide selection of health insurance plans.

"Brokers need fast, accurate information when they call us," says Harris. "That's why my company doesn't have voice mail." Brokers represent specific organizations seeking comprehensive health insurance at affordable rates. They call Benefit Partners for information and rates they can present to their clients. Callers always talk to a live person at Benefit Partners. If their specific rep isn't available, brokers talk to another member of the rep's team who can answer their questions.

Robert Lowcher, an account manager for Time Inc., relies on precall planning, good relationships with customers, and setting priorities to bypass phone tag. Lowcher works with grocery stores and other retailers to distribute Time Warner magazines—*Time, Money,* and *People*—in stores.

"When I meet a new customer, I learn the person's schedule, best times and phone numbers to call, e-mail address and other office telephone numbers. Does my new customer answer the phone? or is voice mail always on? How long does the person take to return calls?"

While Lowcher's customer, the head buyer, is the key decision maker, other members of the buyer's team frequently answer routine questions. When he does need to speak to the head buyer, he says, he limits his questions to those no one else can answer.

Set priorities, Lowcher emphasizes. Before contacting a customer, he puts himself in the buyer's shoes and asks, "How important is this problem? Is it something I must resolve now? or can I address it later when I have time?"

Lowcher recalls an experience when he called a customer at home on a Sunday, which paid off for both of them. "When John F. Kennedy was shot, most people were uncertain if he was dead," he says. "*Time* magazine assumed he had died and planned a memorial issue in his honor. One buyer usually ordered 5,000 copies for his stores, but I knew that this issue would be a big seller.

"I called the buyer at home on a Sunday and left a voice mail message about the special issue. I told him my deadline for ordering extra issues was that evening. He called me back, ordered 25,000 copies and sold 90 percent of them.

"But if I hadn't been looking out for my customer and built a relationship based on trust, both of us would have lost out."

Sometimes, the telephone just isn't enough to put you and your customer in direct contact. Both Harris and Lowcher have developed similar backup strategies based on voice mail, fax, or e-mail, as well as the U.S. Postal Service or Federal Express.

First, leave a concise voice-mail message saying why you are calling, the time, and phone numbers where you can be reached. Also, leave another voice-mail message focusing on the key benefits of returning the call. For example, Harris' reps refer to the group the broker represents. They emphasize lowest cost or being the only service that allows employees to select their own health plan.

Send a fax or e-mail message to your customer emphasizing benefits, deadlines, and the urgency of calling you back. Lowcher requests a return receipt for his e-mail message, hypes the benefits of participating, and reminds customers they will lose out if they don't respond by the deadline. For e-mail, Harris' reps put the name of the broker's group on the subject line. That way, the broker knows they aren't sending junk mail.

If nothing else works, use mail or special delivery services. Harris' reps prepare a new rate quote, underlining or highlighting key selling points. Lowcher relies on Federal Express or another delivery service and requests a return receipt with signature. He often includes a "teaser" such as a prepaid phone card and writes, "We need to talk."

Harris reminds his reps, "We need to show customers the benefit of calling us now. We can't imply a benefit; we must state it."

Lowcher advises other sales professionals, "Build relationships with receptionists, assistants, other department heads, and members of your customer's team. If people know you, they can track your customer down or advise you when to call back.

"Once, I couldn't reach the head buyer. Since I knew the heads of merchandising and other departments, I shared my proposal with them and got their support. Then I left a message for the buyer saying, 'I've gotten the okay from those departments. All I need is your authorization to go ahead."

The telephone isn't always enough. Make effective use of a variety of communication media to make sure you reach your customer and close the sale.

Crucial Skills for Selling by Phone

1. Make it possible for your customers to always reach a live person. Voice mail won't give customers the help they need. If possible, make sure a knowledgeable staff member is always available to help callers.
2. Give customers all your phone numbers and the best time to reach you at each one. Also give them your fax number and e-mail address.
3. Take time to find out key information when meeting a new customer. Learn the person's schedule and e-mail address, as well as all phone numbers and best time to use each one. Does your customer answer their phone?
4. When calling buyers, limit your discussions to important issues only they can answer. Consult other members of the buyer's team for answers to routine and less urgent concerns.
5. Take time to build rapport with your customer's support staff. They will help you locate your customer and advise you when to call back.
6. Set priorities. Before calling a buyer about an "urgent" promotion or other concern, put yourself in the buyer's position. Then ask yourself, "How important is this? Must I solve this problem now or can I wait?"

7. Develop a backup communications system. Consider alternatives such as voice-mail messages, faxes, and e-mail messages, or use a delivery service.
8. Consider "top-down marketing" as a way to avoid phone-tag bottlenecks. Begin by calling the office of the president or CEO. Let the assistant refer you to the right decision maker.

Phone Time Management Skills

Few would argue that the telephone is not a salesperson's lifeline to customers. Yet it can also sap the time reps should be spending on other tasks, such as face-to-face meetings, drafting proposals, and researching prospective customers. If you're finding your phone becoming a permanent extension to your ear, try these time-saving telephone tips from Tom Hopkins' book, *Selling for Dummies*:

1. Set aside a specific time each day to make and take calls.
2. Set a time limit for each call.
3. Write down your objective for each call, put it in front of you during the call, then stick with it.
4. Have all the materials and information you think you might need for each customer within reach before you pick up the phone.
5. Find polite but effective exit lines to help get you off the phone without making the customer feel slighted. For instance, Hopkins suggests saying something like, "Barbara, just one more thing before I hang up...," a statement that indicates you are wrapping up the call without doing so abruptly.

6. Let your customers know when you can be reached by phone. Include this information on your business cards, as part of your e-mail signature, and on your voice mail.
7. If one of your customers is a chatterbox and simply won't let you off the phone, tell him whenever he calls that you're in the middle of something extremely urgent and you'll call him back. Then call him shortly before the time he leaves the office at the end of the day. "You'll be surprised how brief conversations with such people can become!" says Hopkins.
8. Invest in a high-quality headset. That way you can use both hands to quickly find information, pull up a pertinent Web site, sign routine paperwork, or attend to other tasks while you're on the phone.

CHAPTER TWENTY-THREE
Mastering Customer Service

Always Focus on Service

Great selling is all about great service. If your customers leave feeling "sold" rather than "served," they won't feel good about their purchase and they probably won't come back, says T. Scott Gross, author of *Outrageous!* If you want customers for life, follow these tips from Gross:

1. *Remember names.* Using a customer's name, especially if he hasn't been to your store in a few months, has real impact. Gross tells the story of a company that enters its customers' license-plate numbers into a computer. When a customer pulls into the parking lot, a salesperson enters that number into the computer and up pops the name of the customer along with his or her last purchase. That way, regardless of how long it's been since the client was last in, the salesperson can greet the customer with something like, "Good morning, Mrs. Smith! How have you enjoyed that wool suit you bought last fall?" Talk about an impression!

2. *Don't let stupid rules send customers elsewhere.* Gross recalls a month he didn't receive a bank statement and called to get another one sent so he could balance his account. The bank's response: the statement had been sent and because they didn't receive it back, it would cost $2 for them to send another copy. The message Gross heard was that neither the bank nor the post office could possibly be at fault, so Gross must surely have misplaced the statement and should therefore be charged for the effort of sending out another copy. The bank quickly became Gross's former bank, forever losing a customer because of $2.
3. *Never send a customer away without a solution.* This isn't about telling a customer how to fix a problem your company doesn't handle; it's about taking as much of the effort as possible out of the customer's hands. For instance, if you run an electronics store and don't carry the part a customer is looking for, offer to call around to other stores—competitors included—until you locate the part. If you know the nearest retailer is 200 miles away, offer to have your courier pick it up next time he's in that city. Regardless of whether you make a sale that day, you'll likely secure a customer for life.

Using Surveys to Find Out Why a Customer Abandoned Ship

Losing valued customers is unpleasant enough, but not knowing the reason for the defection makes the experience all the worse. You're left wondering, "Was it something I said? Something I did? My personal hygiene?" But if you want to get to the bottom of the customer-defection story, authors Jill Griffin and Michael Lowenstein may be able to help. In their recent book *Customer Winback: How* to *Recapture Lost Customers—and Keep Them Loyal*, Griffin and Lowenstein offer the following guidelines for the gumshoe sales rep:

1. *Start on the inside.* Review the account's history with others in your organization who are familiar with the case. These people may not know everything, but they can often provide a different perspective than yours. Also look at old customer files to see if there are any signs of cause in letters, call reports, or changes in order patterns.
2. *Interview.* Many departing customers will agree to a short exit interview, provided you explain that you merely wish to understand where the relationship went awry, so as to avoid similar problems in the future. Ask whether the decision was based on the quality of merchandise or service, your company's attitude, price, relocation, a poorly handled complaint, or a billing problem. Also inquire whether the customer gave any advance warning of the potential defection. Close by asking whether, if the problems you've identified were addressed, the customer would consider coming back.
3. *Bide your time.* Fresh from the breakup, your newly departed customers may not feel comfortable being frank about their reasons for leaving. Instead of calling immediately upon hearing that a customer is going (which may irritate them all the more as they wonder why you weren't so attentive before), wait a few months and then call. Your chances of getting honest feedback improve, plus the customer will have a better basis to compare the competition's performance to yours.
4. *Look for ill logic.* Sometimes, despite your best detective work, the pieces will still not fit. This may be because the

decision to terminate the relationship was based on emotion and not logic. Customers will rarely reveal such emotional considerations. But the good news is that some emotional decisions may be considered one-time events by customers who later will be willing to rejoin your client list.

Be Invisible to Customers

Great salespeople wouldn't dream of doing a disappearing act on customers, but they do know how to be helpful without being intrusive. To perfect the invisible approach, adopt a more subtle, sophisticated selling style with these ideas and watch more customers and sales appear.

1. *Independent relationships.* An independent relationship shows customers that they're the salesperson's top priority. Though outside factors may affect the customer relationship, invisible salespeople try to maintain independent relationships so they can provide great service under any circumstances.
2. *New focus on customers and salespeople.* Invisible salespeople know a bad customer relationship won't last, so they make every effort to make the relationship rewarding to the customer. Salespeople who are enthusiastic, informed, vocal customer advocates foster greater customer loyalty.
3. *Valuable resources.* By staying on top of industry and technological developments, invisible salespeople become part of the solution to their customers' problems. Stockpile resources (industry publications, the *Wall Street Journal*, the Internet, motivational tapes) and use them to your customer's advantage.
4. *Information access.* The more you know about your customers, the more you can help them. Start by reading your customer's annual reports and company literature, but don't

end there. Use the Internet regularly to research your customers' (and their competitors') companies. Be sure you're on the mailing lists of key players in your buyer's industry.
5. *Shared visions and goals.* To make the customer relationship as productive and profitable as it can be, align your efforts with your customer's goals. Question customers regularly on their biggest problems and challenges, and make sure you understand what they want to accomplish and by when.
6. *Increased expectations.* To make sure your performance is up to par, ask for feedback. Find out with surveys and in conversation if you're meeting your buyer's needs and if you're helping them meet their buyer's needs effectively.
7. *Better mousetraps.* Customers who can't live without your product can't live without the ones who supply it—which puts you in an enviable position. Know which products are most useful to which of your customers. Be on the lookout for new products and services you can provide to help your buyers maintain their edge.
8. *Loyalty.* Invisible salespeople guard their buyers' trade secrets and give smaller customers the same great service and attention they offer bigger ones. Even when their loyalty costs them a sale, they know the long-term returns are worth the sacrifice.
9. *Empowerment.* When you can make decisions on your own, take the initiative, and don't be afraid to speak out on your buyers' behalf. Don't value power for its own sake, but for how it can help you do more for your clients.

Service Energy

An Expert's 12 Tips for Outrageous Customer Service

Today it's not enough just to keep customers happy; with competitors constantly nipping at your heels, you need to keep customers wondering how they ever did business without you. In *Just Say Yes! Extreme Customer Service*, Philip Nulman suggests updates on 12 classic service philosophies to suit the outrageous times we live in.

1. *Outpromise, outdeliver.* Promise a lot and then deliver even more. If customers want it by noon Friday, surprise them with it at the close of work Thursday.
2. *Open at 100.* One hundred percent is the place to begin. If we tolerated just 99.9 percent, then that would mean 14 crashes at O'Hare, 16,000 lost pieces of mail, and 500 botched surgeries a week.
3. *Use your expert ease.* To become and remain the consummate expert, know your stuff, stay on top of industry changes, and always analyze your past performance, looking for ways to improve.
4. *Noteworthy thoughts.* Keep a creativity notebook. Whenever you hear or read of an innovative idea, or you think of one yourself, you'll have a handy note pad to record it.
5. *Keep it fresh.* Maintain a sense of excitement about the journey you're on and continue to dream about reaching your destination.
6. *Cool to be kind.* Imagine your business growing exponentially with each act of unmitigated kindness you perform on your customers' behalf. How will it feel to be number one in your market?
7. *Get with the program.* Create a "personal best" program detailing the actions you will take every day to generate new business.
8. *Separate and unequal.* Divide your tasks into "urgent," "important," and "everything else." Then add to the "urgent" list the following: "Develop ownership of 10 new customers per month."

9. *Race the 4-D.* Make the four D's of time management your mantra: do it, delay it, delegate it, or destroy it.
10. *Opposites attract.* Think about the competition in terms of opposites. For example, stop competing and start creating. Offer value-added service and you create new solutions rather than trying to beat the competition with the same old solutions.
11. *Coach trip.* If you're not an inveterate optimist, consider getting an acting coach to help you develop a more positive business persona. Your business will grow and so will you.
12. *Cut your losses.* Get rid of losers and losing philosophies. They have no place in your business and should never come into contact with your customers.

Essential Readings About Motivation

CHAPTER TWENTY-FOUR
Ethics in Thought and Action

Can You Pass This Test in Ethical Salesmanship?

Below you will find three everyday selling situations. What makes them special is that they potentially involve a risk for unethical action. Please read each situation carefully. Before you answer the question at the end of each example, ask yourself:

(a) Is there an ethical conflict?
(b) What would my manager do in this situation?
(c) What action will I take that is in my best interest and in line with company policy?

Test No. 1: Can You Salvage This Order?

You have been working for two months on an industrial account to obtain a firm commitment for a $185,000 computer system. If you can land the order today, you will become eligible for a quarterly performance bonus of $2,500. To meet your competitor's lower price, your manager decides to give you special authorization to offer your client a $9,000 package consisting of free software, specialized operator training, and extended service contract terms. Similar incentives have been offered on special occasions in the past. You feel that this sweetened offer will bring you below your competitor's rock-bottom price. You know that your customer is a price buyer.

As you drive to your customer, you get tied up in a huge traffic jam. You call your client from your car phone and ask his secretary if it would be okay to come about 30 minutes later than scheduled. She tells you not to worry. As you are ushered into the buyer's office, you greet your customer with smile, ready to announce the good news. He informs you that he signed a contract with your competitor just 10 minutes ago. Upon your insistence, he shows you the bottom line on the signed contract. You realize that by purchasing your system he could have saved as much as $12,000.

> Would you try to reverse your prospect's decision?
> Write your answer in the space below before reading further.

What Guides Ethical Decisions?

The above example illustrates a knotty problem created by conflict in loyalties. You may feel that the customer acted unfairly. You therefore feel justified in your desire to renegotiate the deal. You may feel that because you've invested so much time in this deal, it would be unwise to give up now. You may have already spent the bonus in your mind so why let a competitor take what was already destined to come your way? Why should your customer have to pay a premium if he could save money with your deal? Aren't you supposed to create satisfied customers?

We all offer different justifications for our actions in different situations. Companies that issue written guidelines for ethical conduct covering this particular situation will help the salespeople in the decision-making process.

For instance, marketing representatives working for IBM will find the following directive in the booklet entitled *Business Conduct Guidelines*: "As a matter of practice, a competitor already has a firm order from a customer for an application, we don't market IBM products or service for that application before the competitor has installed." IBM's guideline is clear. Stop selling.

But what if a company does not have such guidelines? What if your sales manager tells "war stories" when he himself has persuaded a customer to call your competitor and cancel the purchase order and return the deposit check? According to experts on ethics, such action has direct consequences on the bottom line. Managers who demonstrate unethical behavior will negatively impact productivity. A two-year study sponsored by the Exxon Education Foundation discovered that companies that practice ethics on a day-to-day basis will enjoy higher levels of productivity. Gary Edwards, executive director of the Ethics Resource Center in Washington, D.C., explained it this way: "People don't want to be ashamed of where they work or what they do. And they won't be productive if they are."

Test No. 2: Can You Create a Win-Win Situation?

As the sales manager of a printing company, you are about to invest in a car-leasing program that involves 18 company cars for your sales staff. Together with your comptroller, you have examined several leasing programs. You have narrowed down your selection to two leasing companies that offer very similar terms. You are meeting with the president of Equilease, a company with which you have never done business before. You know from your own prospect files that one of your sales representatives has tried to call on the purchasing manager of Equilease before to get some of their printing business; however, he could not crack the account.

As you meet with the president for lunch, you gently steer the conversation in the direction of printing services. Because he is very knowledgeable about printing services and prices, you ask him about ballpark prices charged by his existing supplier. You feel that you could provide his company with high-quality service at a better price.

Because the president of Equilease is in a good mood, you think about setting up a win–win situation. You are considering an offer in your mind like: "Let's make this a double win. I'll give you 100 percent of our leasing business, if you'll consider giving us 50 percent of you printing business. Fair enough?"

>Would it be ethical to propose such a deal?
>Write your answer in the space below before reading further.

Principles Guide Thoughts, Not Actions

We asked you not to read further unless you have answered the question above. If you have been tempted to first look at the comments below prior to shaping your "official" response, then you may have been misled by one of the many incentives for unethical conduct. Two major incentives for unethical conduct are (a) the absence of specific rules of conduct and (b) the absence of effective controls.

According to a study sponsored by the Ethics Resource Center, 75 percent of Fortune 500 companies have developed written codes of ethics. The study also revealed that most of these codes (61 percent) consist only of general principles rather than specific rules of conduct.

What's most surprising, however, is that only a few firms have the necessary mechanisms to see that the principles of ethical conduct are upheld. Only 15 percent of the companies surveyed have ethics committees to monitor compliance.

Although published general principles of a company's ethical beliefs are good for public relations, they are fairly useless as a guide for solving everyday ethical conflicts. Without a clear-cut, reality-based guideline and practical monitoring of compliance, the above ethical conflict could put the sales manager and his company at considerable risk.

In essence, the sales manager was seeking reciprocity. The contemplated deal is clearly unethical. In some cases such a deal may be even unlawful. (The Federal Trade Commission Act of 1914 gives the commission broad powers to prevent unfair trade practices and unfair methods of competition.)

Companies aware of their legal and ethical responsibilities protect themselves and their employees from unnecessary exposure.

For example, IBM marketing representatives are urged to follow the specific steps set forth in their Business Conduct Guidelines: "You may not do business with a supplier of goods or services on condition that it agrees to use IBM products or services." Reasonable? Quite. Important? Absolutely.

Remember that your career and the future of your company depends on creating values that last. This depends on making decisions we can live with tomorrow, not on what we might get away with today.

Test No. 3: Can You Call a Spade a Spade?

You are in the very competitive business of selling office machines. You have an appointment with the senior partner of a large medical center. She has already studied several competitive products. Her hot buttons are low operating costs and low maintenance. You know that four competitors have demonstrated their product to your prospect. After you have shown her the benefits of your products, she asks you: "Tell me, what makes your machine better than brand X?"

You restate some of your obvious product benefits and she comes back with: "The salesman with company X told me that they use a special kind of toner that is far superior to what you are using for your machine and that it will increase the lifetime of their machine by 20 percent." You know that this is an obvious lie so you ask: "What evidence did this salesperson give you to prove his claim?" She shows you a customer testimonial letter that talks about how satisfied they were with their machine, but it says nothing about longer lifetime. You reply carefully: "That's the first time I have ever seen a letter praising a brand X machine."

Next, she shows you another piece of paper, it's a chart that graphically illustrates the operating costs of five different brands. The chart says on the bottom "Marketing Research-Brand X, 2006." It shows your machine with the highest operating costs over a five-year period and it shows brand X in the leading position with 50 percent lower operating cost. You are stunned by this unfair competitive comparison. You try to control your temper and think about saying: "They always are much better than we are on paper, but when it comes to reality, we outperform them any time." Would your comment be ethical?

Write your answer in the space below before reading further.

Unfairness Begets Unfairness

Dealing with unfair competition represents a double challenge. On one hand you want to get the order; on the other you want to stop the competitor's unfair practices. In this case, your prospect is using every bit of information to play one competitor against the other to obtain the best deal. What do you do when the fight for business is getting dirty?

First, take notes when you hear a customer's reports about unfair comments made by your competitor. Turn the information over to your sales manager or legal department. Your role is not to pass judgment on the case but to collect the evidence.

Second, do not "knock" the competition, but let the competition knock itself out. It's virtually impossible to build a lasting and profitable business by risking customer trust and confidence on every single deal. Should your customer find out that the operating cost figures were nothing but lies, company X would not be able to sell a single office machine to the medical center in the future.

Reputable companies believe in the lasting power of honesty. Their policies and guidelines reinforce that message to every salesperson. For example, Xerox representatives are bound by ethical guidelines that state: "Make no disparaging statements, directly or by any kind of inference or innuendo, about competitors and their products and services—even if you believe them to be true."

IBM tells its marketing reps: "It has long been the company's policy to provide customers the best possible products and services. Sell them on their merits, not by disparaging competitors, their products or services."

These guidelines are tough, but fair. They were drafted with the clear realization that salespeople are the stewards of their company's reputation.

The absence of ethical guidelines will always create the illusion of safety, yet these illusions are short lived. More than 200 years ago, Thomas Paine wrote about the unethical actions of Great Britain: "A long habit of not thinking a thing wrong gives it the superficial appearance of being right." History proves that appearances are deceiving. It also proves that without ethical conduct, freedom is unsafe.

CHAPTER TWENTY-FIVE
Being a Professional in Every Way

Be Professional Enough to Sell

Have you ever read ads in the help-wanted section of your newspaper that say "Professional Salesperson Wanted – No Experience Necessary"... "Salespeople Wanted – No Soliciting Required"... "Salespeople Wanted – No Canvassing"? What a joke!

How can you sell without soliciting or canvassing? How can you be a professional salesperson without having experience? Observe four typical scenes and draw your own conclusions about what makes a salesperson professional.

Scene no. 1: The salesman "drops in" unannounced. The buyer is on the phone talking to a friend. The salesman overhears the buyer say that "a salesman walked in but he can wait." The agent wastes valuable selling time waiting for the chit-chat to end. The buyer hangs up and says that he doesn't have time to see the salesman today.

Scene no. 2: The buyer tells the saleswoman that her prices are competitive but that she will have to cut them in order to be considered. Reluctantly, she complies only to find that someone who arrived later cut the quoted prices even further in order to get the sale.

Scene no. 3: The salesman shows the buyer a quality product at a reasonable price. The buyer states that the price is too high. The salesman then goes to a cheaper-priced product from another line. The buyer says it is still too high. Eventually, the salesman goes down to the bottom of his "sales grab bag" and pulls out his cheapest product. He makes the sale. Shortly thereafter, however, the buyer tells the salesman the merchandise is shoddy and there is no need to call on him any more. He made the sale but lost the account.

Scene no. 4: The saleswoman makes a successful presentation. The buyer is satisfied with the price and the product or service features. The buyer then states that he must have the product delivered or service completed by an unreasonable date. To get the business, the saleswoman, knowing full well it cannot be done by that time, tells him it can. She gets the sale. And she subsequently loses it and the customer when the product or service is not delivered on time.

In each of these four scenes, the salespeople were willing to lower their standards in order to make a sale. After all, that's the object of selling, isn't it? Yes, the object of selling is to make sales, but earning a buyer's respect while making the sale is what distinguishes the professional from the nonprofessional. Building a long-term relationship creates a true professional who will be able to make a living no matter what territory, economic, and business constraints arise.

It's simple, yet often overlooked. People want to do business with people they can trust. Sometimes, buyers will throw out tests just to determine trustworthiness. There should be no hesitation in giving honest answers.

Beyond honesty, here are some guidelines for salespeople to follow. Proper use of selling time often distinguishes one salesperson from another. It has been estimated that it costs $250 and up for someone to make a sales call. Physical canvassing or just "dropping in" on a prospect or customer belongs to a bygone era.

Qualify prospects first by mail or telephone to make sure that they will honor the salesperson's time. During an appointment, if you feel your time being taken up unnecessarily, excuse yourself by stating you have another appointment to keep and offer to return at a later date. By so doing, you will give the buyer subtle notice that your time is valuable. Sellers should have reasonable, but firm, prices. Changing prices in midstream gives a buyer an image of wishy-washy pricing tactics and a lower image of the firm. There is a difference between negotiating and appearing to have an unstructured pricing policy.

Sell only proven products. One of the most common mistakes made in marketing is trying to substitute an inferior product to compete in pricing wars. It just doesn't wash. Instead, tell the prospect that you could deliver a cheaper product but it wouldn't have the same features or quality of the product being discussed. If the competition wants to practice that type of marketing, the salesperson may lose the sale for the time being but will win a customer in the long run.

False promises about availability will boomerang sooner rather than later. Local advertisers who practice this tactic usually end up in the Better Business Bureau files. A damaged business reputation is difficult, if not impossible, to repair.

Some buyers just may not know of the limitations of your delivery schedule. If the ship from the Far East arrives but once a month, tell the customer that you are out of stock now but can deliver at a future date. It is also a good way to book orders ahead of schedule, and hopefully ahead of the competition.

The sales professional must be taught that he or she cannot be all things to all people. He must be taught that his company, its products or services, and its pricing policies represent a high standard that will not be compromised.

CHAPTER TWENTY-SIX
Working with Your Boss

Managing Your Boss Doesn't Mean Bossing Your Manager

Nine Tips on How to Get Ahead by Getting Along Better

In addition to the skills needed to make a sale (prospecting, presenting, closing, etc.), salespeople also must be proficient in management skills. These include time management, self-management, and even boss management. But managing your boss doesn't mean bossing your manager. It means understanding your boss and managing yourself. Below is a list of action skills to help you take greater initiative and responsibility in your relationship with your boss from Dr. Bob Menoff, president of ODT Associates in Amherst, Massachusetts.

1. *Stop trying to change your boss.* The key to building a better relationship is a willingness to change yourself. Many salespeople underestimate the power they have to improve a situation by changing their own behavior.

2. *Self-knowledge is a key to power.* Personal awareness is just as important as technical competence for your professional success. Self-knowledge gives you the ability to determine the match of styles you have with the person you report to. This lets you take responsibility for the effect you have on your boss and learn how to change it if the effect is not what you desire.
3. *Assumptions about your boss's goals can wreak havoc with the relationship.* Learn specific skills and strategies for making sure you are fully aware of your boss's objectives. Skills needed include: asking clarifying questions, probing for information, and objectively pointing out inconsistencies when tasks seem out of line with stated goals of the department.
4. *Have priorities and make sure yours are in line with those of your boss.* Keep your boss posted on how you've prioritized your work. Failure to understand shifting priorities can cause communication breakdowns and a possible loss of job. Give your boss the chance to reshuffle your priority listing of current projects.
5. *Take responsibility for making the relationship work.* Relationships can often be dramatically improved through the efforts of just one person. Don't indulge in petty resentments. Just because your boss may be older and making 30 percent more than you do, don't leave all the managing of the relationship to him or her.
6. *Take responsibility for the evaluation process.* Learn the skills of receiving a performance review. Plan throughout the year, not just at evaluation time. Clarify expectations early in the evaluation cycle. Solicit feedback (positive and negative) in a systematic fashion.
7. *Become a scientific investigator.* Study your boss's personality, style, and preferences. Pick up on likes and dislikes. Find the best time and manner in which to present information to

the boss. Ask your peers (or even your predecessor) for ideas on how to work with the boss most effectively.
8. *Build on your boss's strengths.* Try not to dwell on weaknesses and shortcomings. Focusing on your boss's negatives will only make things worse. Find something positive and build your strategies on that.
9. *Use psychological judo.* Don't resist your boss's objections. Accept them. Probe and determine the full emotional and factual background. Diffuse resistance by fully understanding the situation from your boss's point of view.

This managing formula applies to all working relationships whether it be between salesperson and district sales manager, or district sales manager and national sales manager, or national sales manager and vice president of sales, and on up the corporate ladder. By learning how to manage your boss by understanding your boss and managing yourself, you can establish better, as well as more productive, working relationships.

How You Can Manage Your Manager

- *Dateline Atlanta*: A sales manager, recently upgraded from rep, persists in functioning as a salesperson. There's no game plan, minimum training and guidance, and poor role definition for staffers.
- *Dateline Toledo*: A manager transferred from a branch is inadequately briefed and prepared for his new duties and responsibilities. He's pretty much at sea in supervising his department.
- *Dateline Boston*: A sales manager experiencing marital difficulties compounded by a drinking problem leaves the 14 reps in his charge floundering.

- *Dateline Phoenix*: A salesperson with wedding plans on her mind feels that a 40-hour-per-week grind in a competitive industry is too heavy a burden. She gripes about overwork and accuses her manager of being disorganized.

Reasons vary, but real or unfounded, staff complaints about the disorganized manager, says Tom Bello, president of Fine Printing Impressions in Boca Raton, Florida, "are an age-old problem that will never go away 100 percent." Having worked every corner of the business for 24 years, he also believes that a key remedial word for the problem is support. "For managers to be really effective," he adds, "they must have adequate backup behind them. Higher-level management, account supervisors, and senior marketing executives must understand that their number one responsibility is to support the sales effort—with all the goal-setting, planning, direction, role definition, and guidance this implies."

Bello, who worked in sales under his company's previous owner, understands and has experienced the problem first hand—confused schedules, inadequate planning, rush work, missing details, poor assignment of duties, you name it. "What I did," he says, "and what I would recommend to salespeople who find themselves in this spot, is to sit down with their boss for a productive meeting on ways and means to improve communication. Not a whining, finger-pointing session, but a discussion sparked by ideas, suggestions, and a genuine desire to see the ship sailing smoothly."

Define the Game Plan

Fine Printing Impressions sales rep Steve Bowers agrees with his boss. "Your manager," he says, "may have no idea the problem exists. I would inquire in a calm, nonaccusatory way about my manager's plans for the days and weeks ahead. What are the goals? Are they clearly expressed? Should these questions disclose an inability to spell out what needs to be done, this in itself could bring the disorganization to light. A rep might say, 'These are the things you want me to work on. Can you rank them in order of importance, so that I will know what comes first and I can address what needs to be done systematically?'"

For the managers who are as smart as they are disorganized, this approach might provoke thought leading to corrective action. It could also bring to light the possibility that it might be you and not the manager who's disorganized, in which case, now may be the time to get help with your problem. Before jumping to conclusions concerning your boss's shortcomings, take time to evaluate your own assumptions, Bowers suggests. He recommends a questioning look at the whole situation: "What is my manager really asking and expecting of me? Do other reps have the same dilemma? If so, how are they dealing with it?"

When should you throw in the sponge? "If your job skills and talents aren't being broadened and used to their full potential, and if there's no way you can change this, it may be time to move on," says Bowers. "Only you can determine a plan of action tailored to your own unique and special needs," he adds. "One thing's for sure. If your boss is indeed at fault, only he can solve the problem. But you can go a long way in helping him to do so and wind up a hero in the process."

Bello raises another key question: "As a sales rep, how heavy a workload can you sustain?" He presents the hard-nosed executive's point of view. "Some staffers simply can't handle being told what to do if they feel too much work and stress are involved. Or they don't have a thick enough hide to deal with all the complications, interruptions, and changes. If that's the case, and if they are worth saving, they should be moved elsewhere in the company."

It could be a tough reality to deal with. But if the shoe fits, you should bear it in mind.

Help Wanted

If you see yourself as a victim of disorganized management, where can you go to seek help? "Your choices are limited," Bowers says. "Go over your boss's head and you may be perceived as a crybaby. The time to take action is when your job performance and career prospects are being hurt by the problem."

If there's a key person who has taken an interest in you, tactfully seeking that executive's counsel could make sense. Get the message across that your chief concern is to do your job right and enhance the company's bottom line. If nothing else, this will be a respected approach.

It is absolutely essential, Bello stresses, to have your role spelled out explicitly. Communication is a two-way street. Accomplishing this is as much the rep's responsibility as it is the manager's.

CHAPTER TWENTY-SEVEN
Keys to Self-Improvement

Is Self-Improvement Part of Your Job Description?

"As long as you are in the career of selling, you must be in a career of training, of learning, of self-development, of getting better." This chapter shares key self-improvement strategies from Jim Evered, president of HRD Services, who has trained (and learned from) more than 30,000 sales and management personnel throughout the United States, Canada, Latin America, Europe, and Asia.

As a sales representative and a professional, you need to carry out a systematic and continuous plan of self-improvement. In the modern world of business and selling, competition is getting tougher and tougher. Competition for jobs is getting tougher; competition for the customer's dollar is getting tougher; the sales ability of your own competitors is getting tougher and tougher.

The only way you can survive is to get better and better and to do it faster than your competitors. Your training doesn't end at the completion of a formal training program—it only begins. A formal program will serve as no more than a launching pad for your training. As long as you are in a career of selling, you must be in a career of training, of learning, of self-development, of getting better. Of course, experience adds greatly to the development of any man or woman, but it also takes a lot of hard study and analysis to be the best you can be.

In addition to the usual sales objectives, establish monthly, quarterly, semiannual, and annual objectives for personal development. These objectives are, of course, above and beyond those activities required by your company. These are the things you plan to do on your own to make yourself more valuable to your company, to your profession, to your family, and to yourself. It is the hallmark of true professionals to constantly seek ways of becoming more professional in their work. It is a means of wringing a full year's learning from each year on the job. There is a vast difference between the salesperson who has 10 years of experience and the one who has "one year's experience 10 times." The one who is capable of making each year a learning experience is in a position to move up the corporate ladder and become a manager of others.

Personal development objectives are often established in very vague, ambiguous terms; for example, "During the next six months I will exercise greater diligence in the performance of my duties and increase my selling skills to become more professional." This nice laudable statement means nothing. Sure it sounds like a nice idea, but it isn't a clear-cut objective.

Any objective, self-development or otherwise, should be established to meet the following five criteria:

1. It must be realistic and attainable.
2. It must be measurable. (Otherwise you don't know whether you met it.)
3. It must be clearly and unambiguously stated.
4. It must provide "stretch." (Otherwise, there's no real growth.)
5. It must be in writing.

Here are two self-development objectives that meet the above criteria:

1. During the next six months, I will read at least three books on professional salesmanship and prepare a brief report on each for my sales manager, including the key point I have applied in selling.
2. Within the next six months, I will have enrolled in and completed a night course in "Marketing Strategy" at a local community college and will have submitted to my sales manager two proposals for means of increasing our market penetration by at least 1 percent.

There are countless ways of improving on the job, but few salespeople actually do anything other than what's required by their company. Sales managers have a perfect right to expect personal development objectives from each of their salespeople on a regular and continuing basis. It is part of the manager's strategy for developing their sales personnel and bringing them to a promotable level.

Regardless of your manager's requirements, it is to your benefit to grow in the job. There is a direct correlation between personal growth and increased earnings. It makes the sales representative more valuable to his or her customers. There is greater self-satisfaction in becoming more professional. It often gives the salesperson a big edge over the competition and produces more sales volume.

Another method of achieving self-growth is to constantly experiment with new techniques and ideas. The salesperson never lived who had the perfect way of presenting a product to a customer. A highly successful technique for one sales representative can be a complete failure for another. What one person would say to close a sale may not work at all for another. There really isn't any full explanation for it—it just happens. Differences in personality, language, communications techniques, and a host of other factors cause it. There are no 10 perfect rules for selling that will work for everyone, and for every 10 techniques you try, perhaps only one of them really works for you. This means that if you don't try all 10 of them, you will never know which one is the winner for you. You will have to try at least 100 techniques to find the 10 winners. Then you discard the 90 that didn't work and hone the other 10 to a fine edge. It is through a program of self-development that you find ideas to try, so you can separate the successful ones.

A truly professional sales representative is never satisfied with his or her selling techniques. As good as they are, there are always better ones, stronger ones, more successful ones to be found. The amateur doesn't bother. Amateurs affect everyone; they are never bad enough to fire and never good enough to promote. They clog up the pipeline of corporate growth and personal growth.

Here are some of the sources and activities to which a sales representative can turn to build a continuing program of self-development:

1. Libraries and bookstores full of excellent books on salesmanship, marketing, and related subjects.
2. Participation in a local Toastmaster or Toastmistress club.
3. Night courses or correspondence courses at a local college or university.
4. Correspondence courses from the American Management Association.
5. Reading trade publications and magazines.
6. Specialized courses periodically offered in your area (e.g., The Dale Carnegie Course).
7. A multitude of cassette tape programs on a full spectrum of job-related subjects.
8. Special seminars offered on related subjects.
9. Subscribing to sales publications (such as the one you are reading now).
10. In-depth discussion of selling techniques with professional sales people from other industries.

There is a limitless supply of sources for growing in the job if you are really serious about it. But the key is involvement. No one can learn for you—you must do it alone. It is your life; it is your career. Will self-improvement be part of your job description during the next 12 months? or are you going to get the same year's experience—one more time?

CHAPTER TWENTY-EIGHT
Stress-Reduction Basics

One morning I awoke with a gripping pain in my chest. It was 6 a.m., time to begin my regular daily routine. I was sure the pain was the result of something I'd eaten the night before, or perhaps the six sets of sit-ups I had done. I was sure if I could just get up and walk around, I would be fine.

People tell me I don't do anything just a little bit, but plunge into everything I do in life. The pain continued. Not wanting to be alarming, I remained silent with my family.

On the way to work in my car I felt some relief. However, once there I began to experience even more pain. At that point I became frightened.

I shared my concern with a co-worker who had himself experienced some heart problems. He immediately advised me to call my doctor who in turn told me to go straight to the hospital.

Panic set in. I believed I was having a heart attack. In fact, I was sure I was dying. However, after a series of tests, the doctors gave me different diagnosis: heart attack, no, stress, yes.

I left the hospital with more questions than answers. How did I get into this mess? Could this happen to me again?

I never saw myself as a stressful person. Selling is like play for me. I always thought of myself as easy going. I roll with the punches, I'm flexible, and I have high rejection tolerance. The diagnosis belonged to someone else. Surely they were wrong about my chest pain.

Subsequently, I read everything I could get my hands on about dealing with stress and concluded that stress is a very personal condition. The ingredients that created stress for me may not have created stress for someone else. How could I manage stress? Should I continue with my current pattern of behavior and suffer the apparent consequences, or should I implement a strategy for change? Slowly, over a period of time and by trial and error, I decided to take the following plan of action to reintroduce balance into my life.

1. *Think health.* One of the most significant motivators in my professional life has been the attainment of excellence, frequently at any cost. That cost has included my health. In the past, exercise was a four-letter word that spelled HURT. But, it is an important ingredient in balanced living. Frequently, I would exercise for two hours and then forget about it for months. I now exercise regularly, doing fun things. I walk, take ballet lessons, and sometimes I even listen to exercise tapes.

2. *Lower sights.* I am now setting more realistic goals and consistently working toward them. My tendency was to set highly unrealistic goals and focus upon them exclusively. I now try to be motivated by them rather than be obsessed with them (this incorporates balance between work and play). This past summer, one of those benefits was enjoying four-day weekends at the seashore. I allowed myself to enjoy the benefits of my labor knowing that I had earned them.

3. *Build self-esteem.* Like many salespeople, I had devoured my share of "self-help materials." But reading is not enough. It was time to practice the principles. One of the major reasons I had pursued professional excellence was because deep down

I wasn't sure I could achieve and thus sought constant affirmation. Fortunately, I have several people who affirm me and now I eagerly accept and thrive on that affirmation.

4. *Cap hours.* Was I spending or investing my time? I approached my work with a basic belief: "The longer the hours, the greater the success; the longer the hours, the greater the stress." I realized that once I decided I was going to work only eight hours a day, I immediately removed a great deal of anxiety from my life. My question was no longer how long would I work, but rather how could I work most effectively in that predetermined time frame? This process also moved me from the constant preoccupation with my work life and enabled me to relax enough for my creativity to surface and function. My question is no longer when will I have time to smell the roses but rather how do they smell today?

5. *Face fear.* I was terrified of failure, but it took me a long time to admit it to myself. I decided to concentrate on affirming my strengths rather than trying to cure all my weaknesses. I now have the freedom to ask myself some difficult questions: "What is the worst that could happen if I don't make this sale? How can I profit from either success or failure?"

I realize each day that my action plan is not a magic formula. I have come to the personal conclusion that stress is as much a question of my attitude as my action. My failure to address the problem at the attitude and action levels will only create additional stress for me. I certainly have not eliminated stress in my life, but I have experienced a good deal of relief since I've chosen to use it as a creative force rather than letting it victimize me.

I have had no recurrence of chest pain, and my attitude toward life has changed drastically. The visit to our local hospital gave me a new gift ... the gift of life lived more fully.

CHAPTER TWENTY-NINE
Always Strive for Success

Be Destined for Success

Motivational Experts Weigh in on What It Takes to Send Your Achievement Levels Soaring

Inspect the average sales rep's shelves, backseat, or file cabinet and you're bound to run across an assortment of cassettes, books, pamphlets, and other paraphernalia all dedicated to one subject: achieving success. Salespeople are legendary for building veritable arsenals of motivational materials.

Yet despite absorbing the collected wisdom of many of the top success gurus, the average sales rep remains just that—average.

So why is it that so many sales professionals become stifled in their achievement levels or plateau before reaching the rarefied air of success they aspire to? Part of the problem, experts agree, is that too frequently people define success exclusively in financial terms while giving short shrift to the other critical dimensions that make up a successful life. This focus is generally supported by many of our cultural values—consider how often we hear revelations of the disastrous private lives of otherwise "successful" business professionals or celebrities.

As a result, explains Dr. Jan Gault, psychologist and author of *The Mighty Power of Your Beliefs*, people who operate within such a narrow definition of success often find themselves ill-equipped to handle financial setbacks.

"Say you have a string of rejections, you lose a big sale, or you have to file for bankruptcy," she says. "You're going to feel like a failure if you're just hanging success on that one dimension of your life. If we can't put these unwanted outcomes into perspective with the rest of our lives and values—family, health, personal relationships, and so forth—this can throw us into a state of depression."

Gault adds that, while we don't always control outcomes and economic conditions, we do always have control over how we perceive and interpret these outcomes. "That's why our definitions of success are critical, for our mental health as well as for our ongoing success," she says.

Pride in Yourself and Your Profession

Here are truths that will help you focus on important aspects of pride that are associated with the sales profession.

Customers sense a salesperson's attitude and they reflect that attitude back to the salesperson. If you project fear or prejudice, your customer will seem fearful and prejudiced toward you. If you are feeling broke or discouraged, your customer will complain loudly about how bad business has been and how tight money has become. On the other hand, if you are positive and upbeat, your customer will respond accordingly.

If you think that what you do for a living is boring or unimportant, your customers will probably agree with you. But if you take pride in your career and demonstrate that pride every time you make a sales presentation, your customers will react positively to what you have to say. In short, you can control how your customers respond by controlling how you feel. Your attitude makes all the difference between success and failure with customers.

Customers naturally feel more prosperous when they have positive cash flow. It is also only logical that when people feel prosperous, they are more likely to buy. How does this relate to the issue of pride and your attitude about yourself? It's simple! If you feel prosperous, people will want to do business with you. If you feel poverty-stricken, they won't. If you see yourself as a person who is so important that people should rearrange their schedules to accommodate you, they will sense that importance and will probably make the necessary rearrangements.

If you have high standards and stick to them, you will generate trust. Always be your own person. Don't compromise your principles or change your offer to accommodate your customer because you think it will somehow help you make the sale. Whenever you compromise your standards, you accomplish only two things: First, you convince the customer that you really did not know what was best for him in the first place. Second, you convince the customer that you did not care what was best for him. The customer concludes that you were only interested in closing the sale, not in meeting needs or solving problems.

The customer does not want to be right but does want to know that you are right and that you know what is best for him. Also, the customer wants to be assured that you have enough integrity to do whatever is best for him. Don't bother trying to use rusty psychology on your customers. Talk straight!

Take pride in:

- Your ability to help other people improve their lives. Salespeople help companies build equity, shareholder value, profits for growth and research, and the cash to make investments in the future.

- Your honesty. The handshake and signature of every salesperson should always be an unshakable and inviolable bond of trust.
- The contribution you make to the success of the company where you work.
- Your appearance. Dress like a successful celebrity, wearing the finest clothes you can afford.
- Your knowledge of selling, your product or service, your company, and the market you serve.
- Your reliability and punctuality. Keep every promise you make. Be someone that everyone can count on.
- Your ability to sell. Don't look for a job selling products or services that move quickly and easily, and don't spend all of your time seeking out the easiest customers in your territory.
- Your skills. When you say, "I am a professional salesperson," expect respect.
- Finally, take pride in your reputation. Don't be satisfied with 100 percent delivery. Be satisfied only when you have achieved 100 percent customer satisfaction!

Credits

The following chapter sections were originally published in *Selling Power* and written by...

...*Lloyd Allard*
"Pride in Yourself and Your Profession"

...*Daryl Allen*
"Be Invisible to Customers"

...*Steve Atlas*
"Telephone Selling"
"Crucial Skills for Selling by Phone"
"E-mails That Sell"
"How to Use E-mail to Build and Maintain Relationships"

...*Heather Baldwin*
"Always Focus on Service"

...*Ray Dreyfack*
"Ready to Close"
"How You Can Manage Your Manager"

...*James F. Evered, CSP*
"Is Self-Improvement Part of Your Job Description?"

...*Malcolm Fleschner*
"Buyer Be Where?"
"Dale Carnegie's Strategies for Winning Friends"
"Keys for Selling New Products"
"How to Turn-Around Difficult Customers—and Yourself"
"Cold Calls, Hot Selling"
"Prospecting and Voice Mail Tips That Work"
"Mirror, Mirror, on the Call"
"Price Squad"
"Chase Down the Evaders"
"As Time Goes—Buy"
"Service Energy"
"Be Destined for Success"

...*Joseph Fred, Jr.*
"Be Professional Enough to Sell"

...*Gerhard Gschwandtner*
"Can You Pass This Test in Ethical Salesmanship?"

...*William F. Kendy*
How to Use Negotiation to Increase Sales

...*Joan Leotta*
"Price versus Value"

...*George J. Lumsden*
"Do You Clean Up or Give Up on Follow-up?"

...*Dr. Bob Mezoff*
"Managing Your Boss Doesn't Mean Bossing Your Manager"

...*Andrea J. Moses*
"Overcoming the Eight Biggest Negotiating Mistakes"

...*Judith Rosen*
"Cracking the Vault"

"What Voice Messages Actually Get Customers to Call You Back?"

...Alison Smith

"Outselling Your Competition"

...Betsy Wiesendanger

"Using Nonverbal Skills to Build Strong Customer Relationships"

...Kim Wright Wiley

"Executive Travel Tips"

...Renee Houston Zemanski

"Powerful Tips to Disarm Toxic Remarks"

"Ten Tips to Effective Cold Calling"

"Packing Persuasion in Your Writing"

Index

A

Action
   ethics, 187–194
Active-voice verbs
   proposals, 154
Administrative assistants
   voice mail, 89
Alternative contracts, 87
Atmosphere
   salespeople, 13
Attitudes
   salespeople, 14, 216–217
Audio training
   sales skills, 53

B

Books
   motivation, 75
Boss
   executive point of view, 203
   game plan, 202–203
   priorities, 200
   strengths, 201
   working with, 199–204
Business
   to business shows, 115
   future, 106
   power of failure, 106
   profiles, 100
Buying decisions
   customers, 3

C

Call backs
   voice mail, 140
Capping hours, 213
Clarity
   proposals, 154
Clients. *See* Customers
Closing essentials, 165–170
Coaching
   managers, 13–14
   one-on-one sales skills, 54
   personal motivation, 77
   sales knowledge improvement, 31
Cold calls, 123–128
   effectiveness, 124–126
   excuses, 123
   follow-up strategies, 151
   giving up, 126
   goals, 124
   ratios *versus* numbers, 125
   success strategies, 126–127
   trade shows, 116
College course
   sales skills, 54–55
Communications
   keys to strengthen, 143–145
   nonverbal
      negotiations, 110

Company profits
   negotiations, 114
Competition
   outselling, 99–101
   potential clients, 100
   pricing information, 99
Complaints
   follow-up strategies, 149
Compliments
   giving, 145
   receiving, 145
Conflicts
   resolution, 15
Consulting
   sales knowledge improvement, 31
Content
   reflecting, 144
Contracts
   alternative, 87
Conversational style
   proposals, 155
Cost-cutting, 86
Co-workers
   stress, 211
Customers
   abandoning ship, 178–180
   difficulties, 103–108
   objection, 161
   empowerment, 181
   expectations, 181
   focus
      salespeople, 180
   follow-up strategies, 147

immediate calling, 179
information
    access, 180
invisibility, 180–183
loss, 178
memory
    follow-up strategies, 151
motivation, 165–167
    industry data, 166
    small orders, 166
    upselling, 168–170
needs
    proposals, 156
organizations
    decision makers, 92
potential
    competition, 100
relationships, 105
    nonverbal skills, 105
    salespeople, 103
service
    mastering the art, 177–183
    tips, 181–183
speech
    objection, 162
toxic remarks, 104–106
voice mail, 176

D

Decision making
    customer
        organizations, 92
    negotiations, 111
    salespeople, 87
Decisions
    ethical guidance, 188–189
Difficult customers
    objection, 161
Dilenschneider Group, 85
Disorganized
    management, 204
Distribution
    low cost, 97

E

E-mail
    advantages, 130
    existing ideas, 130
    sales process, 129
    sales tools, 129–134
    telephone prospects, 131
Employees
    profile, 100
Enthusiasm
    manager, 6
Ethics
    action, 187–194
    decisions
        guidance, 188–189
    salesmanship, 187
    specialized operator training, 188
    thought, 187–194
Evaluation process
    self-responsibility, 200
Eye contact, 127

F

Failure
    business future, 106
Feelings, 144
Follow-up strategies, 147–151
    cold calls, 151
    complaints, 149
    customer memory, 151
    customers, 147
    referrals, 151
    relationships, 150
    salespeople, 149
    selling opportunities, 150
    suggestions, 149

G

Game plan
    boss, 202–203
Gatekeepers, 85–90
Gestures
    salespeople, 108

Goals
    salespeople, 13–14
Greeting
    first move, 128

H

Help wanted, 204

I

Improvement
    checklist, 33
    opportunities
        identification, 11
    plan
        development, 11–13
    motivation, 74
    sales motivation
        recommended actions, 75–78
Industry data
    customer motivation, 166
Industry trends
    marketing, 98
    sales, 98
In-house sales training
    sales skills, 53–54
Internet age
    voice mail, 139

J

Job sources
    supply, 209

K

Knowledge. *See also* Sales knowledge
    improvement checklist, 33
    improvement plan, 30
    review, 17–34, 19f–29f
    skills, 4–5
    successful
        competition, 3
    travel tips, 118

L

Leads
  cultivation, 91–94
  development, 91–94
  generation, 91–94
  positive feedback, 128
  prospects, 125
Letters. *See* Sales letters
Listening
  reflective, 143

M

Managers
  ability, 201–203
  challenges, 96
  coaching, 13–14
  disorganized, 204
  enthusiasm, 6
  poor sellers, 5
  process repeat, 12–13
  review, 10
  review meetings, 9–10
  sales knowledge, 4
  salespeople goal motivation, 61
  success factors, 3–16
Marketing
  industry trends, 98
Motivation. *See also* Customers
  books, 75
  creation, 5
  experts, 215
  improvement plan, 74
  personal coaching, 77
  rating scale, 63f–73f
  review, 61–79
  rewards, 77
  salespeople, 5, 61–79
    goal, 61
    managers, 61
  speakers, 76
  tapes
    objection, 158

N

Negotiations, 109–114
  company profits, 114
  decision-makers, 111
  goals, 109
  mistakes, 110–114
  nonverbal communications, 110
  price
    justification, 112
    lowering, 112–113
  sales, 109
  strategies, 114
New-product selling, 97
Nonverbal communications
  negotiations, 110
Nonverbal skills
  customers
    relationships, 105

O

Objections, 157–163
  difficult customers, 161
  motivational tapes, 158
  open-ended questions, 162
  price list, 160
  price squad, 158–160
  Reagan administration, 157
  speech to customers, 162
  strategies, 157–158
  tips, 158–160
Objective
  self-development, 206
Obstacles
  ways for tackling, 89
One-on-one coaching
  sales skills, 54
Open-ended questions
  objection, 162

Outside sales training courses
  sales skills, 54

P

Performance
  recognition, 9
  salespeople, 16
Personal best program, 182
Personal coaching
  motivation, 77
Personal Selling Power Certificate of Sales Achievement, 13
Persuasion
  proposals, 155
Persuasive Paradigm, 155
Phone
  e-mail prospects, 131
  skills
    selling, 174–175
  tag
    bypassing, 171
    voice mail, 172–173
  time management
    skills, 175
Postcards
  trade shows, 116
Potential customers
  competition, 100
Power
  underestimating, 110–111
Price
  negotiations, 112–113
  squad
    objection, 158–160
  vs. value, 160
Pride, 216
Problem solver
  sales manager, 6–15
Product knowledge, 17, 95–98
  salespeople, 17, 106
Profession
  pride, 216–218

Proposals
    active-voice verbs, 154
    clarity, 154
    conversational style, 155
    customers' needs, 156
    familiar words, 153
    persuasion, 155
    positive outcome identification, 156
    positive outcomes, 156
    sentences, 154
    solutions, 156
    tips for writing, 153–156
    unnecessary words, 153
Prospects
    leads, 125
Psychological judo, 201

Q

Quality rating scale, 7–8
Questions, open-ended objection, 162

R

Reagan administration objection, 157
Referrals
    follow-up strategies, 151
Reflective listening, 143
Review meetings
    managers, 9–10
Rewards
    motivation, 77

S

Sales
    barricades, 87–89
    e-mail, 129–134
    industry trends, 98
    in-house training
        sales skills, 53–54
    leads
        steps to generate, 93–94
    motivation
        improvement, 75–78
    objectives, 206
    outside training
        courses
            sales skills, 54
    skills, 53–55, 199
        audio training, 53
        college course, 54–55
        in-house sales training, 53–54
        one-on-one coaching, 54
        outside sales training courses, 54
        video training, 63
Sales knowledge
    improvement
        coaching and consulting, 31
        outside training programs, 32
        reading assignments, 31
        salespeople, 31
        sales training, 31
        self-paced training, 32
    managers, 4
Sales letters
    benefits, 136
    definition, 135
    getting attention, 135–137
    paragraph length, 136
    positivity, 137
    visual appeal, 136
Sales manager
    problem solver, 6–15
    review, 6–7
Salesmanship
    ethical, 187
    specialized operator training, 188
Salespeople
    appearance, 218
    atmosphere, 13
    attitudes, 14
    contributions, 218
    customers, 103, 180
    decision-making, 87
    empowerment, 181
    follow-up strategies, 149
    gestures, 108
    goals, 13–14
    managers
        motivation, 61
    honesty, 218
    information access, 180
    knowledge, 17–18, 218
        improvement, 31
        rating scale, 18
    motivation, 5, 61–79
    natural born, 4
    objectively rating scale, 8–9
    performance, 16
    recognition, 9
    product knowledge, 17, 106
    progress, 12
    punctuality, 218
    quality rating scale, 7
    rating scale scores, 11
    reliability, 218
    reputation, 218
    selling results, 169
    skills, 218
    standards, 217
    trust, 217
    upselling, 169
    wisdom, 6
Sales Team Performance Summary, 34
Sales Team Performance Summary Skills, 58–59
Sales training
    sales knowledge improvement, 31

Self-development
 objectives, 206, 207
 program, 208
Self-esteem
 development, 212
Self-growth
 achievement, 207
Self image, 217
Self-improvement
 keys to, 205–209
Self-knowledge, 200
Self-paced training
 sales knowledge
  improvement, 32
Self pride, 216–218
Self-responsibility
 evaluation process, 200
Selling
 follow-up strategies, 150
 inside, 179
 new-product, 97
 opportunities, 150
 philosophies, 183
 phone skills, 174–175
 power, 32, 55
 results, 169
 service, 177
 skills, 4, 37
  goals, 37–38
  rating scales, 38
 stages, 125
 stress, 212
Sidetracking, 14
Skills, 4–5
 improvement check
  list, 56–57
 improvement plan, 52f
 needed sales, 199
 nonverbal customers
  relationships, 105
 review, 37–54, 39f–51f
Speakers
 motivation, 76
Specialized operator
 training
  ethical salesmanship, 188

Speech
 customers, objection, 162
Strategies
 negotiating, 114
 objection, 157–158
Stress
 co-workers, 211
 reduction, 211–213
 workplace, 213
Success
 manager, 3–16
 strive, 215–218

T

Tapes
 motivation, objection, 158
Teasers
 voice mail, 173
Telephone. *See* Phone
Teleselling skills, 171–176
Territory management, 119
Thought, ethics, 187–194
Time management skills
 phone, 175
Tips
 customer service, 181–183
 disarming toxic
  remarks, 104–106
 objection, 158–160
Touch Campaign, 101
Toxic remarks
 customers, 104–106
 disarming, 104–106
Trade shows, 115–116
 cold calls, 116
 postcards, 116
Trade Show Training Inc., 115
Training, 205
 in-house, 53–54
 sales, 31
 sales skills, 54

self-paced, 32
specialized
 operator
  ethical salesmanship, 188
 video, 63
Travel success, 117–119
 keys, 117–119
 knowledge, 118

U

Upselling
 customer motivation, 168–170
 salespeople, 169

V

ValPak, 129
Value *vs.* price, 160
Verbs
 active-voice,
  proposals, 154
Video training
 sales skills, 63
Voice mail, 139–142
 administrative
  assistants, 89
 call backs, 140
 customers, 176
 emergency updates, 142
 Internet age, 139
 key skills, 142
 phone tag, 172–173
 target account
  identification, 140
 teasers, 173
 urgency to reach, 141

W

Wisdom
 salesperson, 6
Workplace
 stress, 213

About the Author

A dual citizen of both Austria and the United States, Gerhard Gschwandtner is the founder and publisher of *Selling Power*, the leading magazine for sales professionals worldwide, with a circulation of 165,000 subscribers in 67 countries.

He began his career in his native Austria in the sales training and marketing departments of a large construction equipment company. In 1972, he moved to the United States to become the company's North American Sales Training Director, later moving into the position of Marketing Manager.

In 1977, he became an independent sales training consultant, and in 1979 he created an audiovisual sales training course called "The Languages of Selling." Marketed to sales managers at Fortune 500 companies, the course taught nonverbal communication in sales together with professional selling skills.

In 1981, Gerhard launched *Personal Selling Power*, a tabloid-format newsletter directed to sales managers. Over the years the tabloid grew in subscriptions, size, and frequency. The name changed to *Selling Power*, and in magazine format it became the leader in the professional sales field. Every year *Selling Power* publishes the "Selling Power 500," a listing of the largest sales forces in America. The company publishes books, sales training posters, and audio and video products for the professional sales market.

Gerhard has become America's leading expert on selling and sales management. He conducts webinars for such companies as SAP, and *Selling Power* has recently launched a new conference division that sponsors and conducts by-invitation-only leadership conferences directed toward companies with high sales volume and large sales forces.

For more information on *Selling Power* and its products and services, please visit www.sellingpower.com.

SellingPower
Open More Doors. Close More Sales.

Maximum Impact

ALSO AVAILABLE IN THE SELLING POWER LIBRARY

Great Thoughts to Sell By • The Psychology of Sales Success
Be In It to Win • Sales Stories to Sell By • Secrets of Superstar Sales Pros

for any Sales Career

McGraw-Hill books are available at special quantity discounts to use as premiums and sales promotions, or for use in corporate training programs. For more information please contact us at bulksales@mcgraw-hill.com, or contact your local bookstore.

Visit us at www.sellingpower.com/bookstore. *Available everywhere books are sold.*

Certificate of Sales Achievement

This is to certify that

_____

has achieved significant progress during the past three months in the following areas:

Sales Knowledge Improved by _____ %
Selling Skills Improved by _____ %
Motivation Improved by _____ %

_____ _____ _____
Gerhard Gschwandtner   Sales Manager   Date

SellingPower